NRA Hunter Skills Series

BOWHUNTING

Produced by the NRA Hunter Services Division. For information on the Hunter Skills Series, NRA Hunter Clinic Program, or becoming a volunteer hunter clinic instructor, contact the National Rifle Association of America, Hunter Services Division, 1600 Rhode Island Avenue NW, Washington D.C. 20036-3268. Telephone (202) 828-6240.

Library of Congress Catalog Card Number: 90-083402

Main entry under title:
Bowhunting—NRA Hunter Skills Series

ISBN 0-935998-63-X

HS5N5403 (paperback)   HS5N5449 (hard bound)

ACKNOWLEDGEMENTS

Authors

Mike Strandlund, Managing Editor, *Bowhunting World,* former Program Specialist, Editorial Productions, NRA Hunter Services Division

M.R. James, Editor *Bowhunter,* First Vice President Pope and Young Club

Karl J. Gunzer, Jr., Program Specialist, NRA Hunter Skills Department

Editors

Mike Strandlund, Managing Editor, *Bowhunting World,* former Program Specialist, Editorial Productions, NRA Hunter Services Division

Karl J. Gunzer, Jr., Program Specialist, NRA Hunter Skills Department

Production Managers

Earl W. Hower, Program. Manager, NRA Hunter Skills Department

Doug Pifer, Resource Specialist, Editoral Productions, NRA Hunter Services Division

Illustrator

Doug Pifer, Resource Specialist, Editorial Productions, NRA Hunter Services Division

Co-Authors and Review Committee

Len Cardinale, National Archery Association Master Coach and Member, National Bowhunter Education Foundation Board of Directors

Dr. Dave Samuel, Professor of Wildlife Biology, West Virginia University, Member, National Bowhunter Education Foundation Board of Directors, and Vice President, American Archery Council

Dave Staples, Past President Professional Archers Association and Member, Archery Hall of Fame Board of Directors

Jim Norine, Director, NRA Hunter Services Division
Barry Winner, Program Manager, NRA Hunter
    Education Support Services Department
Robert L. Davis, Jr., Program Manager,
    NRA Youth Hunting Skills Department
Dave Messics, Program Specialist,
    NRA Hunter Skills Department
Kitty Beuchert, Assistant Director, NRA Women's Issues
    and Information Division and former Program
    Manager, NRA Hunter Information Department
Billy Ellis, Noted Bowhunting Lecturer, Writer and
    Trust Officer Pope and Young Club
Dave Woodward, Chief of Information and Education,
    Tennessee Wildlife Resources, President, National
    Bowhunter Education Foundation, and
    Past President, Hunter Education Association

The National Rifle Association of America is grateful
for the contributions made by the preceding persons, by
the National Bowhunter Education Foundation, and the
government agencies and organizations credited
throughout this book.

Photo Credits

Front Cover Photo by **Mike Strandlund**
Back Cover Photo by **Joe Workosky**

NRA Hunter's Code of Ethics

I will consider myself an invited guest of the landowner, seeking his permission, and conduct myself so that I may be welcome in the future.

I will obey the rules of safe gun handling and will courteously but firmly insist that others who hunt with me do the same.

I will obey all game laws and regulations, and will insist that my companions do likewise.

I will do my best to acquire marksmanship and hunting skills that assure clean, sportsmanlike kills.

I will support conservation efforts that assure good hunting for future generations of Americans.

I will pass along to younger hunters the attitudes and skills essential to a true outdoor sportsman.

Archery Safety Rules

The fundamental rules for safe archery/bow handling are:
- Always keep the bow with a nocked arrow pointed in a safe direction.
- Never draw a bow with nocked arrow until ready to shoot.
- Do not nock an arrow on the bow string until ready to use.
- Always keep field points or broadheads covered until ready to use.

When using or storing a bow, always follow these rules:
- Be sure the bow is safe to operate.
- Know how to safely use the bow and its equipment.
- Use only the correct arrows and equipment for your bow.
- Never use alcohol or drugs before or while shooting.
- Store bows and other archery equipment so they are not accessible to unauthorized persons.
- Never dry-fire a bow.

Be aware that certain types of archery equipment and many shooting activities require additional safety precautions.

TODAY'S AMERICAN HUNTER

I f you're a hunter, you're one of 20 million Americans who love the outdoors, have a close tie with traditions, and help conserve our natural resources. You know the thrill and beauty of a duck blind at dawn, a whitetail buck sneaking past your stand, a hot-headed, bugling bull elk. With your friends and forefathers you share the rich traditions of knowing wild places and good hunting dogs. Your woodsmanship and appreciation of nature provide food for body and soul.

And through contributions to hunting licenses and stamps, conservation tax funds, and sportsman clubs, you are partly responsible for the dramatic recovery of wildlife and its habitat. Hunters can take great pride–and satisfaction that only hunters know–in the great increases of deer, turkeys, elk, some waterfowl, and other species over the last century.

Your involvement with the National Rifle Association of America is also important to promote conservation and sportsmanship. In NRA, concerned hunters and shooters work together for laws and programs of benefit to the shooting sports. Most important is the education of sportsmen through programs like the nationwide Hunter Clinic Program operated by the NRA Hunter Services Division. Through the program and the Hunter Skills Series of how-to hunting books, America's already admirable hunters can keep improving their skills, safety, responsibility, and sportsmanship to help ensure our country's rich hunting traditions flourish forever.

CONTENTS

WELCOME TO BOWHUNTING

We have a spectacular history in archery. The bow and arrow are indelibly etched into mankind's evolution. Shots made in the name of love, lust, war, peace, vengeance, honor, hunger, pride and sport stretch all the way from the caveman's bearskin robe, to the golden arrow in a velvet case—and even here and now, to the draping of a medal around our Olympic champion's neck, or the tagging of an outstanding trophy animal taken by bow and arrow.

The style, form and technique of successful archery from then to now, surprisingly, has stayed about the same, at least in principle.

Our long-dead kinsmen used the hunting bow to sustain life. It provided food, clothing, and shelter, along with defense from enemies. It was a way of life. And it still is. While modern bowhunters no longer depend on the bow for survival, those who choose to carry a bow afield are reliving a time in history when personal skills and simple tools were all-important. No thoughtful person who bowhunts can help but remember and be affected by the memory and meaning of such a long and rich hunting heritage.

The spread of interest in bowhunting in America can be traced to a book written by a pair of brothers from Georgia—Maurice and Will Thompson. After the Civil War, they found themselves denied the use and possession of firearms. The *Witchery of Archery* tells how they used the bow and arrow to live off the land through the mid 1800's.

Early in the 20th Century another twosome, Dr. Saxton Pope and Arthur Young (see left photo), did much to popularize bowhunting as a sport. Pope's 1923 book, *Hunting With the Bow and Arrow,* further promoted archery hunting.

Perhaps no name is more closely identified with introducing hunters to archery than that of Fred Bear (see page x). In 1933 he founded Bear Archery, and later his worldwide hunting adventures were shared by millions through films, books, and personal appearances. Modern bowhunters owe a debt of gratitude to Fred Bear's creative genius and promotional efforts.

These men, and many lesser-known but equally involved

bow and arrow enthusiasts have contributed much to the growth of bowhunting. By the early 1980s nearly 2 million men and women were legally licensed to bowhunt in the United States. Today, with the hunting bow widely recognized as a very efficient and humane sporting tool, bowhunting is an increasingly popular outdoor pastime.

Photo Courtesy Bear Archery

Although deer are the primary targets of the modern bowhunter, virtually all species of big and small game have been successfully hunted by archery enthusiasts. Many consider bowhunting to be the ultimate hunting challenge.

The purpose of this book is to help you learn about hunting with a bow and arrow. Whether you're new to archery, new to hunting, or experienced at both sports, this book will help provide you with safe, successful and enjoyable days afield with an age-old hunting tool.

It takes time and effort to become a proficient bowhunter. First, choose equipment that suits your needs, is capable of meeting your hunting goals, and can be mastered with practice. Second, get to know your equipment until you understand what it will and won't do, until the act of drawing and releasing each arrow becomes automatic. Third, learn your personal limitations and effective shooting range. Fourth, learn about the animals you plan to hunt and study effective methods of taking them in an ethical, humane manner. Only then should you consider buying a license and heading into the field.

Part I
The Basics of
Bowhunting

Photo by Joe Workosky

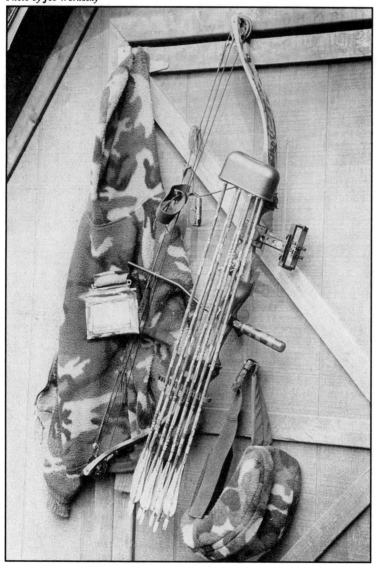

CHAPTER 1

THE HUNTING BOW

Prehistoric man first used crude bows for hunting over 25,000 years ago. Searching for new challenges and seeking contact with his hunting heritage, modern man carries precision-manufactured hunting bows as he trods woodland trails in quest of game.

Photo by Mike Strandlund

Many hunting bows have changed very little over the years. Pick up a modern-made, straight-limb longbow and you're holding a bow quite similar to the weapon used by English soldiers in the Middle Ages. Handle a custom-made recurve bow with laminated limbs of wood and fiberglass and you're holding a bow closely akin to the wood, horn, and sinew laminated bows used by Turks 1,000 years ago. Only the compound bow, with its cables and pulleys and eccentric wheels or cams, is a recent innovation in bow design and development.

Whichever bow you ultimately select, your choice will be based on several factors centered around you and your preferences. While there are differences in makes and models of hunting bows, they are actually quite similar in design and performance. Each requires a shooter's muscles to pull a nocked arrow into shooting position. Each depends on the

Today's hunting bows combine the best features of historical archery equipment and modern technology.

3

shooter's ability to deliver the arrow to its intended target. And each bow has essentially the same components: a handle riser section with hand grip and often a sight window, flexible upper and lower limbs and, finally, a bowstring with some sort of nock locator attached. Later in this chapter we'll examine the various types of hunting bows in greater detail, noting their inherent advantages and disadvantages. Now let's focus attention on you and what you have to consider in selecting the hunting bow that's right for your individual needs.

The Right Bow for You

Are you left- or right-handed? Most often you'll choose a hunting bow accordingly; however, some right-handed shooters have a dominant left eye, and vice versa. On occasion this can lead to shooting difficulties that can best be overcome by switching bow hands and sighting with your dominant eye. Shooting practice, and a simple eye dominance test, will quickly determine whether you should shoot a bow held in your left or right hand.

To determine your dominant eye, first focus on a small, distant object. Cup your hands at arm's length, forming a small opening between your thumb and forefinger through which you can see the object. Slowly draw your hands toward your face, keeping the object in sight between your hands. Your hands will eventually be drawn toward one eye—your dominant eye.

Ideally, your dominant eye and hand will be on the same side of your body. If you are right-handed, and your right eye is dominant, hold the bow in your left hand, and vice-versa. If there is a conflict, it may be wise to experiment until you find the best way of shooting.

Draw Length and Weight

You'll also need to determine your draw length. Bows come in various draw lengths; a short or medium-height person may have a 27-inch draw, for example, while a taller or longer-armed individual may have a 30-inch draw. To find your true draw length, pull a bow to shooting position and measure the distance from the bowstring's nocking point to the back of the bow (the side facing away from you). All compound bows made today are rated according to Archery Manufacturers Organization's draw length standards. Longbows and recurves are not made according to draw length; each is manufactured to

Photo by Mike Strandlund

Selecting the right bow is important in finding enjoyment and success in bowhunting. Get expert advice for choosing a bow with the right design, draw length, draw weight, and other features to fit your personal needs.

a certain poundage required to draw the bow 28 inches. The weight is stamped or written somewhere on the bow.

This poundage, or bow weight, is another important consideration in your bow selection. There are many varying opinions on the subject. Probably the most common advice given beginning bowhunters is: "Shoot the heaviest bow you can pull comfortably and shoot accurately." This advice is good in many respects. A bowhunter who uses a bow that is too heavy cannot achieve his potential for consistent accuracy. A bow that is unnecessarily light has minimal speed and a greater arrow trajectory, which harms accuracy and arrow penetration.

Most modern hunting bows pull between 55 and 70 pounds and, with the right shot placement, are capable of downing any North American big game. Bows that pull as little as 35 pounds are acceptable for deer-size game if they are legal for deer hunting in your state or province, but should be used only for sure shots and short-range shooting—20 yards or less. A few hunters, who practice regularly and stay in shape, use bows of 75 or 80 pounds. Rarely does a bowhunter have the capability or need for something heavier.

The final judgments in bow selection are subjective ones. A parallel may be drawn to selecting an automobile from the many sizes, colors, and models available. Individual taste varies. The look and feel of a hunting bow will, for some, be as important as its brand name and performance history. And since all products of comparable quality may perform basically the same function, this aesthetic consideration should not be

discounted. A positive self-image builds confidence that breeds more confidence. In bowhunting, a sport more mental than physical once the basics of shooting a bow are mastered, confidence is a universal ingredient in any veteran bowhunter's recipe for consistent success.

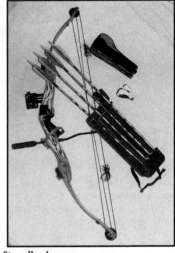

Most modern-day hunters use compound bows although each year many discover—or rediscover—the appeal of traditional gear after getting in-

Photo above by Karl Gunzer Jr., below by Mike Strandlund

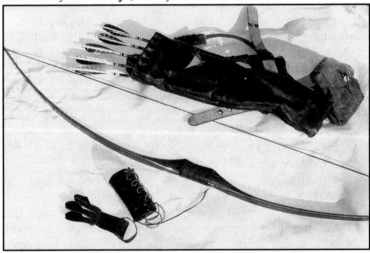

The different types of bows used by archers today reflect different approaches to bowhunting. Some bowhunters prefer high-tech equipment and related accessories. Others prefer traditional longbows and gear. Still others prefer a compromise between these extremes, such as using recurve stick bows with sights or shooting compounds instinctively.

volved in bowhunting, mastering the compound, and searching for new challenges. Considering all your options will ensure you realize the most enjoyment from the sport of bowhunting.

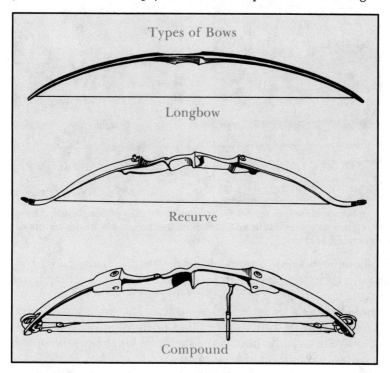

Types of Bows

Longbow

Recurve

Compound

Longbows and Recurves

The so-called stick bows—longbows and recurves—have long proved their effectiveness in taking game. Considering their long history, it is likely that stick bows have accounted for more bagged game than any other hunting tool used by man. Today many bowhunters continue to use them, preferring their clean lines and simplicity over mechanical compound bows and the many gadgets available to the modern bowhunter.

Most bowhunters think of the longbow as a much more primitive design than a recurve. Recurves are much more popular today, though longbows, extremely rare a decade ago, have seen a remarkable increase in popularity.

Stick bows are the logical choice for archers who prefer to shoot without sights. There is considerable divergence of opinion among some archers whether a longbow or a recurve is best-matched to man's instinctive shooting ability.

Photos by Mike Strandlund

The last decade has seen an upsurge in the use of longbows. These bows are quiet, reliable and efficient hunting tools in the hands of practiced archers.

Longbows tend to transmit more "shock" to the bow hand than a recurve when the arrow is released. Very short recurves create some finger pinch on the string hand, which some shooters believe is a deterrent to accuracy. The extra length of a longbow may be a hindrance in a few hunting situations. Arrows are invariably shot off the shelf of a longbow, while some recurves have elevated arrow rests.

Actually, there is little practical difference in performance between longbows and recurves. They shoot arrows with similar velocity and accuracy; performance depends mainly on individual bow design and construction. Assuming the bow is tuned, performance deals primarily with two factors: stacking and cast.

Stacking is the increasingly hard pull as the bow approaches full draw. The best stick bows have the least amount of stacking. Ideally, the bow should increase in poundage uniformly as the string is pulled.

The problems with a bow that stacks badly are that it is unpleasant to shoot and is difficult to shoot consistently. If the last inch of draw increases 10 pounds, for example, any slight variation in draw length will vary the arrow's point of impact.

A bow's cast is how well it springs back on release. A bow's shooting velocity is determined not only by how much energy it stores (the bow's poundage) but also by how efficiently it releases that energy (the bow's cast). A half-dozen bows of identical weight shooting identical arrows will probably have six slightly different velocity readings. The bow with the highest velocity has the best cast. It is the bow with the best combination of materials, design, and construction.

Photo by Mike Strandlund

Recurve bows were standard among bowhunters from the 1940s until the advent of the compound bow in the early 1970s. They have seen renewed popularity today.

The most basic stick-bow design is the self-bow, a longbow carved from a single stave or two staves spliced at the handle. This is generally a very inefficient design with bad cast and stacking, though traditional purists often prefer them. Most modern longbows and recurves are made of laminated wood and fiberglass.

There are a few other modern design changes to improve performance and versatility of stick bows. Many manufacturers and custom bowers offer take-down stick bows, which are not only lightweight but break down for compact transporting and packing. A few bows have reinforced tips that can handle the stress of Fast-Flight strings—a bowstring with very little stretch that increases a bow's velocity somewhat. Price and quality vary considerably among stick bows; if possible, try before you buy.

Advantages of Longbows and Recurves

Many bowhunters find that stick bows agree with their idea of what bowhunting should be. There are also practical advantages that stick bows have over compounds:

- **Less weight to carry.** Longbows and recurves are generally much lighter than compounds, even when mounted with a bow quiver and its complement of arrows.
- **Fewer performance problems.** Minus moving parts and the more complex design of compound bows, stick bows present fewer potential headaches.
- **Ease of sighting and shooting.** Most traditional shooters

aim and release instinctively. This simple method takes much less time than using a sight and may be an advantage in a hunting situation.

Photo by Mike Strandlund

Simplicity and reliability under adverse conditions are among the stick bow's attributes.

- **Ease of tuning.** Good arrow selection, a few twists of the bowstring, and minor adjustments of the nocking point and contact point are usually all that's required to fine-tune a stick bow. Additionally, a stick bow seldom goes out of tune in the field.
- **Attainable accuracy.** Stick bows shoot every bit as accurately as compound bows. Differences between bow types can be traced directly to the shooter's style and skill, not the bow itself.

Combine these advantages with the simple, clean lines of a hunting bow created from beautifully crafted exotic woods, and it's apparent why some bowhunters still prefer the longbow or recurve. Aesthetically appealing and undeniably effective, stick bows remain a link with hunting history in today's high-tech, increasingly complex world.

Compound Bows

Until the advent of the compound bow in the late 1960s, the bowhunter's choice was limited to recurves or longbows. While some stuck with their stick bows, most bowhunters experimented with compounds and converted.

H. W. Allen changed bowhunting forever when he patented his strange-looking bow design in the mid-1960s. The Allen compound bow and others with their unusual array of wheels, pulleys, and cables modernized an ancient weapon and sparked a new interest in bowhunting that continues to this day.

Hailed by some as a creative innovation and denounced by others as a mechanical abomination, compound bows caught on despite protest. Within a decade they were legalized for use by bowhunters in every state.

Besides featuring a reduced holding weight, compounds let speed-conscious bowhunters shoot lighter hunting arrows. Bow weights being equal, the reasoning went, a lighter arrow flies faster and flatter than a heavier arrow. Faster arrows get to the target quicker. Flatter arrow trajectory increases effective shooting range by partially compensating for yardage miscalculations.

Actually, compound bows operate on the same principle as stick bows. When any bow is drawn into shooting position, the energy from the shooter's muscles is transferred to the bow's limbs where it is stored until the arrow is released. At this instant, the stored energy is transferred to the arrow where it becomes kinetic energy—energy in motion—until impact.

The draw weight of your bow, your draw length, and the bow itself all affect the amount of energy stored and released. The greater the amount of kinetic energy released, the

Photo by Mike Strandlund

The vast majority of today's bowhunter's use compound bows with sights and other shooting aids. Modern equipment produces greater arrow speed and penetration, and helps the archer gain a high degree of shooting accuracy.

deeper your arrow will penetrate, all else being equal. Thus, in the days when stick bows were the only choice for bowhunting, using heavier-pulling bows made good sense. Today, the sophisticated design of the compound bow gives bowhunters several other options to consider.

What to Look for in a Compound

Different types and brands of compound bows offer different performance features. Often, a bow buyer must choose between tradeoffs—for each advantage you seek, there is usually a disadvantage.

Photos Courtesy Hoyt U.S.A., Pachmayr, and Oneida Labs

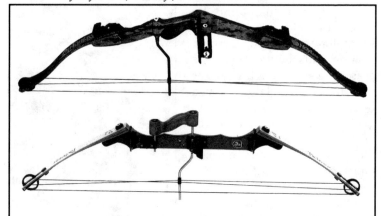

Compound bows today are made in a variety of designs with variations in mechanics, limbs, handles, and other features.

One of the first things a potential buyer of a compound bow will notice is the wide range of prices. Currently, compound bows cost from under $100 to over $500. Can you expect to get what you pay for in performance? For a beginner, usually not. It is advisable to start with a moderately priced bow.

Features that you'll be considering when buying a bow include the amount of let-off it provides. Let-off ranges from about 40 percent to over 65 percent, with most bows in the 50 to 65 percent range. More let-off lets you hold at full draw longer, but may limit the bow's velocity and degrade accuracy.

Like recurves and longbows, compounds have varying levels of "stability," which refers to how sensitive they are to slight variations in shooting style and how conducive they are to accuracy. This is largely determined by design and balance.

Compound bows of different designs and brands also have different levels of efficiency, reliability, durability, and available features.

Parts of the Compound

As mentioned earlier, all bows share three basic parts: the handle, the limbs, and the string. In recent years there have been many innovations in the compound bow and archery accessories, with the goal of increasing arrow speed and accuracy. The modern compound bow used by today's average bowhunter is much more complicated than the "barebow" used by old-time archers and traditionalists of today.

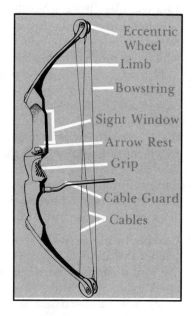

Eccentric Wheel
Limb
Bowstring
Sight Window
Arrow Rest
Grip
Cable Guard
Cables

Following is a list of the components of a compound bow and their variations:

Handle—Compound bow handles are generally made of wood, magnesium, or aluminum. The main advantage of a metal handle is that its strength gives durability and allows it to have a sight window cut deeply past center, which allows the arrow to shoot in a straight line "through" the handle rather than around the handle. Wood handles are warm and lightweight, but lack the strength and durability of metal.

Test-shoot a bow before buying to be sure that the handle suits your shooting style. You may find that the sight window is not large enough for a full range of pin adjustment on certain models. Some shooters prefer thick bow grips, though many get better accuracy with smaller grips, which limit inadvertent torque you might put on the bow as you release the string.

The shape of a compound bow's handle can have some bearing on its performance. A handle that curves inward toward the string effectively shortens the draw length. This may add stability but decrease the bow's dynamic energy potential a bit. A handle that curves greatly outward has the opposite effect.

Beyond these factors, choice of handles is largely personal taste. Many bows are sold mainly on the basis of the handle feel appealing to the buyer.

Limbs—Some limbs are still made of laminations consisting of wood and fiberglass. Most compounds have solid or laminated limbs made with fiberglass, carbon, and various synthetics, which are more durable than wood laminates.

The difference in performance between the different types of limbs is insignificant, but each style has advantages and disadvantages. Laminated limbs are a bit more efficient than solid limbs, mainly because they have less mass to absorb energy that would otherwise be transmitted to the arrow. They require much more workmanship than solid limbs, however and are thus more expensive. They are lighter to carry than solid-glass limbs, but have shorter lives and are more apt to break unexpectedly or twist. Their performance and durability can be affected by temperature changes and moisture.

Compounding system—The cable and pulley system used to propel the arrow—the workings of the compound—is where the real difference between bows lies. The two predominant types available are the two-unit round wheel and cam type, which will be discussed later. Many older compounds have four round wheels.

Most compounds today are of the split limb design, with pulleys located in a split at each limb tip. Older and less expensive compounds have their wheels hung from metal brackets at the limb tips. The split-limb design is more aesthetically appealing and lighter in weight, which makes the limbs more efficient.

There have been several unconventional designs marketed without the standard wheels at the limb tips. The only unorthodox compound design that has seen good success is a brand of compound bow with levered limbs and the pulleys on the handle of the bow.

The efficiency of these mechanics and the amount of resistance within the system determines a bow's speed compared to other models of similar draw weight. The design of the compounding system will also determine how smoothly the bow draws, its adjustability for draw weight, and other factors.

Round Wheel or Cam?

The shape of a compound's eccentric wheels—round or oval—creates considerable pro/con discussion in many bowhunting circles. Simply put, round-wheel compound bows are smoother and easier to draw than a cam bow of the same weight, and

Photo by Karl Gunzer Jr.

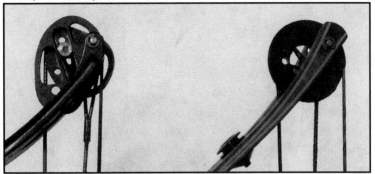

Round wheels (right) are quiet and smooth shooting, but generally don't store as much energy as cams (left).

people tend to shoot them more accurately. Generally, round-wheel bows are quieter to shoot than bows with cams. Cam bows, first introduced in the early 1980s, are designed to store more energy than round-wheel compounds and therefore shoot a faster arrow. Specially designed high-energy cams can generate even more arrow speed. Unfortunately, arrows can absorb only so much energy and what doesn't transfer to the arrow dissipates into the bow's limbs, cables, bowstring, and riser. Unless the cam bow is well designed and well constructed, breakage problems may occur. Early cam bows were plagued with split limbs, broken cables, and strings that couldn't stand up to the stress. Today, most cam bows are quite dependable thanks to redesigned and reinforced limbs, cables, and cams.

Perhaps the best benefit of cam bows is their ability to produce good arrow speed at relatively light draw weights. But when bowhunters insist on shooting lightweight arrows out of heavy cam bows in an attempt to generate tremendous arrow speeds, damage to their bows may still result.

Advantages of the Compound

Compound bows are standard in bowhunting; they're here to stay. Earlier we noted some advantages they offer. Following are a few more good reasons for their popularity:

- **Speed and energy.** Generally, compound bows shoot arrows faster—much faster for many newer compounds—than stick bows. This is for two reasons. The mechanics of compound bows make them generally more efficient than stick bows; that is, for each pound of energy you put

Compound bows are the choice of most bowhunters because the bow's draw weight, let-off and arrow speed enhance the hunter's effectiveness.

into them as you draw, you get more energy out of them in faster arrow flight. Another reason compounds are generally faster than stick bows is that arrows shot from compounds usually don't need to be as heavy as arrows shot from traditional bows. When the identical broadhead-tipped hunting arrows are used in speed tests between compounds and stick bows, differences are not as noteworthy.

- **Let-off.** Picture yourself in a favorite stand watching a nice buck walk slowly into shooting range. As he moves behind a tree 14 yards away, you come to full draw and anticipate the shot as he steps into the clear. But suddenly the deer stops behind the tree with only his head and rump showing. His vital area—the heart/lung area—is screened. You can't shoot. You must hold at full draw and wait for the animal's next move.

If you're using a 60-pound recurve or longbow in this situation, you're at a distinct disadvantage if the buck stays behind the tree for any length of time. While your 60-pound compound bow typically relaxes its weight by one-half when pulled into shooting position, your stick bow remains at peak weight. Obviously, you can hold 30 pounds or so at full draw much longer than 60 pounds and this example underscores the major advantage compounds offer the bowhunter.

- **Adjustable models.** The adjustable weight of compounds holds appeal for many shooters. For example, a person can start practice with his bow set at 45 pounds until he builds his muscles. Later, with a few turns of an Allen wrench, he can increase the poundage and have the same bow set at 60 pounds for hunting by the time opening day rolls around. Experienced archers can better tune their bows because of this same adjustability. Most compounds offer adjustable draw lengths as well as adjustable weights.

- **Ease of use.** Generally it takes a beginner less time to gain hunting accuracy with a compound bow than with a stick bow. Compound shooters usually use sights that, at fixed distances, offer an advantage.

- **Selection and price.** Walk into an archery shop and you can select a compound bow from among dozens of brands and hundreds of models. You can check out the inventory and test-shoot bows before plunking down your money and heading home with a new bow in hand. Compound bows in virtually every size and weight, priced to fit any budget, are as close as the nearest archery shop.

- **Variety of design.** Compound bows, whether fitted with round wheels or cams, come equipped with laminated or solid fiberglass limbs and risers of wood or metal. Generally, solid glass limbs are stronger and more durable than composite wood/glass laminations, and there is no appreciable difference in accuracy where limb material is concerned.

- **Accessories.** Many compounds have a cable guard that holds the cables away from the arrow fletching upon release. These also help quiet a bow. Predrilled holes for bow sights and quivers--as well as stabilizer bushings—are standard offerings on compound risers. Some models have molded hand grips to fit any shooting style.

Your choice of hunting bow remains a largely personal decision. Most bowhunters understand that it is the man holding the bow—not the bow itself—that counts in bowhunting. Today both stick bows and compounds are seen in the hands of North America's top hunters.

The more you can read on the subject and the more bows you can examine—and shoot—the better off you'll be. This is where a knowledgeable archery dealer who knows bowhunting and the equipment can offer valuable advice and provide answers to questions you may have. Also, talking to experienced bowhunters at an area club or shooting range can prove beneficial. Beware of individual prejudices and bias; all dealers and bowhunters have opinions that may not be completely objective. Listen attentively, accept advice when it's offered, and carefully weigh what you hear and read. Then, when the time comes to pick your bow, select what you want, what you're convinced is right for you.

Bow Accessories

Most bowhunters use one or more devices on their bow to aid accuracy, bow performance, or convenience. Following is a list of the major bow accessories.

Arrow Rest

At first glance the arrow rest may seem like an insignificant component of a bow. But because it has a direct effect on the accuracy of the bow, it is one of the most important. Most compounds are factory-fitted with a simple plastic arrow rest. Many bowhunters replace this with a high-performance arrow rest that allows them to tune their equipment for optimum consistency in shooting. The effectiveness of an arrow rest depends mainly on how well it "gets out of the way" of the arrow, interfering little with its takeoff and flight.

These specialized rests come in several designs. Among the most popular among bowhunters is the flipper style, usually used with a cushioned pressure button. The flipper consists of an arm that flips out of the way as the arrow passes. The pressure button is a spring-loaded plunger which provides "give" as the arrow shaft passes the bow handle.

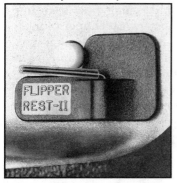

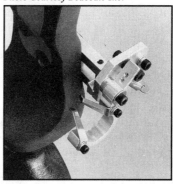

High-performance arrow rests are preferred by most bowhunters because they improve consistency in arrow flight and aid in tuning bow and arrows.

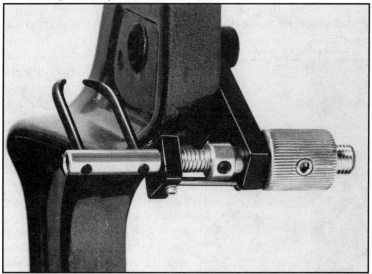

Flippers are classed among the shoot-around rests, which means the entire arrow passes around them as it launches. Another style of rest is the shoot-through type, designed for one of the feathers or vanes to pass through the two or three components of the rest. Another style is the launcher rest, which consists of two prongs that support the arrow shaft on the bottom. The fletching passes on either side of a launcher rest's prongs.

While there are other styles of arrow rests, the flippers, shoot-throughs, and launchers are standard among today's bowhunters. Each has advantages and disadvantages. Flipper/plungers are sturdy and dependable but not as precise as the other types. Shoot-throughs and launchers tend to be sensitive and are designed mainly for archers who use mechanical string releases.

Within each category of arrow rest are design variations with different features that offer different levels of performance, durability and other attributes. Bowhunters should look closely at arrow rests and try several to find the one that best suits their shooting and hunting style.

Overdraws

Some bowhunters conscious of arrow speed have turned to overdraw bows for faster arrows with flatter trajectory. Overdraw systems have been available for many years; however, in the mid-1980s they enjoyed new-found attention with compound shooters. Since they allow a shorter (thus lighter) arrow to be used, they can add perhaps 10 percent to the speed of any given bow. High-speed hunting bows give animals less time to react between the instant of arrow release and impact. They also make range estimation somewhat less critical. On the negative side, accuracy may suffer with overdraws, especially if mechanical releases aren't used. The lighter arrows, though faster, have less energy than full-length arrows and do not penetrate as far. Some hunters believe overdraws are noisy to shoot and dangerous since the broadhead is drawn into proximity just above the shooter's bow hand. Although these points may be debated, there is little doubt some overdraw systems—along with ultralight arrows can be a deadly combination.

Photo Courtesy
Precision Shooting Equipment

An overdraw brings the arrow rest closer to the shooter, allowing him to shoot arrows that are shorter. The shorter shafts are lighter, achieving greater speed and flatter trajectory.

Photo Courtesy Saunders Archery Co.

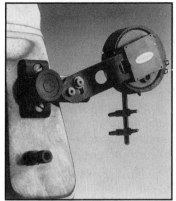

Photo Courtesy Cobra Mfg.

Photo Courtesy Keller Mfg.

Photo Courtesy Ole Norm's Inc.

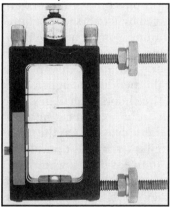

Bow sights come in an array of designs with different functions and features. The most popular is the multiple-pin sight, with pins at varying elevations corresponding to different yardages.

Sights

While compound bows are not factory-fitted with sights, some type of aiming device is an integral part of the bow. Most compound shooters use sights to help place shots consistently.

Like arrow rests, bow sights come in a wide variety of designs. By far the most popular among bowhunters is the sight-pin design. This consists of a rack of about four to six pins mounted vertically on the handle riser. After test-shooting and adjusting his sights, the archer simply chooses the right pin for his yard-

21

age, places it on the target, aligns it with his anchor point, and releases when ready.

There are many types of sight pin designs. The best pin sight system for bowhunters has sturdy, easily adjustable pins, a wraparound guard to keep pins from getting knocked out of adjustment, and a detachable mounting system so the entire sight unit can be removed and replaced quickly with no need for readjustment. This is especially convenient while traveling and the bow must be dismantled to fit in a flat case.

While the vast majority of bowhunters use a sight-pin system like that described above, some prefer a different approach. Some hunters, especially those who use very fast bow/arrow combinations, use only one or two pins, changing their sight picture slightly to cover a wide range of yardages with fewer pins. Crosshair sights—similar to sight pins but with intersecting wires instead of pins—are preferred by archers who believe they are more precise. Treestand hunters sometimes use pendulum sights, a single pin that swings as you raise or lower your bow, automatically adjusting for variations in yardage. Working on a principle similar to the pendulum sight is the manually-adjusting sight, in which the shooter calculates yardage and lines up an indicator with an index coinciding with the correct yardage, which places a single crosshair at the right elevation. Still other archers prefer bow scopes—optical devices using either crosshairs or luminescent dots for aiming.

Most sights can be used in conjunction with a peep sight—a device intertwined with the bowstring, which the shooter looks through and aligns with his pins or crosshairs. Some peep sights use an elastic band connected between the peep and the upper limb, which aligns the aperture in front of the eye each time the bow is drawn.

Other Accessories

Many accessories have been developed to enhance the performance of a bow or adapt it better to hunting. Stabilizers—long weights that screw into the front of the handle—minimize bow movement on the release, aiding accuracy. Bow quivers keep arrows in a convenient place. String silencers muffle the sound of the shot by absorbing string vibrations. When walking, brush buttons keep the bow from getting hung up by preventing twigs and grass from getting stuck between the string and bow limb. Slings make it easier to carry a bow on long walks, while wrist straps keep you from dropping a bow on release.

CHAPTER 2
ARROWS AND POINTS

The arrow is more important than the bow. That's a vogue saying among experienced bowhunters. It may sound simplistic, but it holds a lot of truth. Make no mistake about it: Your choice of arrows is one of the most important equipment decisions you'll make as a bowhunter. Equally important is choosing what to use on the business end of your hunting shaft. Unless your arrows are matched to you and your bow, you won't get the accuracy needed to deliver an arrow to your target. And unless your hunting head is razor-sharp, well-designed, and durable, you won't have an arrow that flies straight or cuts cleanly for the quick kills that all bowhunters should strive for.

Although there are several types of arrow material and design, all arrows consist of the same basic components.

- **Shaft**
- **Head**
- **Nock**
- **Fletching**

Photo by Mike Strandlund

Using the right arrows is crucial for good accuracy and penetration. There are many factors to consider in choosing the types of shafts to buy and what to put on their ends.

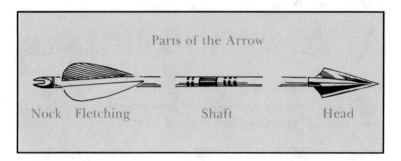

Parts of the Arrow

Nock   Fletching   Shaft   Head

Shafts

The shaft, or body of the arrow, must be the right weight, length, and stiffness for the bow and the shooter. Most important is stiffness, or spine. For optimum accuracy, an arrow must be neither too stiff nor too flexible, or it will fly awry as it leaves the bow.

When the string is released, it transmits a tremendous amount of energy to the arrow. An arrow with correct spine actually flexes around the arrow rest or bow handle before correcting itself after leaving the bow. An arrow with no flex will graze abruptly along the arrow rest and be thrown off course—to the left for a right-handed shooter. A shaft with too much give will bend too much and fail to correct its flight as it leaves the bow.

Arrow shafts are made of aluminum, wood, fiberglass, and composites. Since it affects accuracy so much, the design and construction of the shaft should be carefully considered.

Aluminum

Aluminum is by far the most popular shaft material in use today. This is true in target archery and bowhunting alike, although such was not always the case. First introduced before World War II, aluminum arrow tubing was nearly three decades away from general acceptance and popularity. In the

Photo Courtesy Coleman Arrow Mfg.

Aluminum is by far the most popular material for arrow shafts, and has been since the late 1960s. Today, many are dressed up with camo patterns.

1940s and '50s, it was prohibitively expensive. Not until the late 1960s and early '70s did the durable but lightweight aluminum arrow catch on.

Of the many reasons for aluminum's widespread popularity, uniformity heads the list. No other arrows come from the factory as uniformly matched in straightness, spine, and physical weight—factors necessary for the consistent accuracy competitive archers and bowhunters seek. In addition, quality aluminum stands up well to the normal wear and tear of practice and field use. Although the once-popular fiberglass shaft and modern day composite shaft materials may endure more abuse, aluminum arrows are long-lived and tougher than many people believe.

Like wood, aluminum bends, and may require occasional straightening, either by hand or machine. The procedure slightly weakens the shaft wall and repeated efforts to straighten a bent shaft can produce a weak arrow that may be inaccurate or dangerous to shoot. Cracked arrows should be immediately discarded. Some bowhunters routinely break split or damaged shafts prior to throwing them away. Such action may prevent accidents if the old arrows are found and shot again.

Photo by Karl Gunzer Jr.

One advantage of aluminum shafts is that slight bends resulting from an errant shot can usually be straightened.

Unlike wood, aluminum does not warp and is generally unaffected by adverse weather. It is not unusual for a set of aluminum alloy arrows to last many years. Some bowhunters have collected numerous big game trophies with a single arrow shaft, replacing only the fletching and broadhead as the seasons pass.

Early metal arrow shafting came from the factory with a shiny finish that reflected light like a mirror. It was necessary for bowhunters to use dull-colored paint and steel wool to camouflage their hunting arrows. Later, anodized aluminum shafting appeared in a variety of color shades. And today's aluminum hunting arrows feature camo patterns popular with many bowhunters.

Manufactured to precise tolerances, today's aluminum arrows are produced in varying grades of metal quality in a variety of shaft sizes and spine weights. With only basic information and minimal experimentation, any bowhunter can easily select the best arrow to suit his personal taste and needs.

Wood

Wood was the first arrow shaft material and it remains an excellent choice for bowhunting. Despite rumors that wood arrows can't be used in compound bows, properly spined wood arrows may be shot from any modern-day hunting bow. Further, many traditional shooters favor cedar shafts and their link to the past over the more popular aluminum arrows used by most bowhunters.

"Cheaper" is a term frequently used when comparing wood with other arrow materials; however, a dozen custom-made wood arrows commonly cost a buyer more than a like amount made of any other arrow material. Do-it-yourself arrow builders can make wooden shafts for less money, but a bowhunter shopping for quality wood shafts, matched and spined and treated, had better be prepared to pay extra dollars.

Perhaps the biggest problem with wood arrows is their lack of uniformity and consistency. Spine and weight can vary greatly, even when arrows are machine-produced from the same block of wood. Additionally, raw shafts must be sorted for straightness and it generally takes considerable effort to find or create a matched set of cedar arrows.

On the positive side, inexpensive wood arrows may be made or purchased for stump shooting or small game hunting, where a broken or lost shaft is no big deal. Also, wood is easier to

Photo by Richard P. Smith

Some bowhunters prefer the romance or economy of wood arrow shafts.

straighten than aluminum and there are some wooden shaft shooters who insist wood is more forgiving when a sloppy release or similar shooting error occurs.

Wood will warp, especially if untreated, and proper storage is mandatory. Wood arrows also weaken with age and repeated use. Shooters should constantly check and discard any arrows showing signs of weakness. It's also smart to check for cracks after each shot, since a cracked arrow could splinter the next time it's released and drive part of the shaft into a shooter's bow hand.

People who have a draw length of 32 inches or more will be unable to shoot wood arrows since they are unavailable in longer sizes. Regardless, the vast majority of bowhunters will be able to shoot wood arrows if they wish.

Fiberglass

Once popular in many bowhunting circles, the durable and comparatively heavy fiberglass shafts are rarely found today. A solid fiberglass fish arrow and hunting arrow with a fiberglass shell and cedar core are notable exceptions. Some long-time bowhunters may continue to use fiberglass shafts they've shot since the 1950s and '60s when glass arrows were common.

Durability is the most obvious benefit of fiberglass arrows. If straight at the end of the manufacturing process, a glass shaft will remain straight for the rest of its life. Unfortunately, not all fiberglass arrows are perfectly straight to begin with and, consequently, they cannot attain the accurate arrow flight needed in bowhunting.

Glass shafts also lack the versatility of aluminum, which comes in many weights within a given spine range. For example, a bowhunter with a 65-pound bow and a 30-inch draw may have one or two choices of suitable fiberglass shafting; however, the same person wanting to use aluminum arrows may have his choice of half a dozen shaft sizes and weights spined to shoot well from his hunting bow.

Composites

Graphite- or carbon-composite arrow shafts are yet another option. No other material can offer more spine at less weight,

Photo by Karl Gunzer Jr.

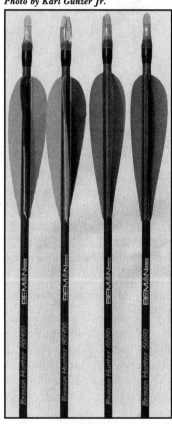

Light, strong carbon composite arrow shafts have increased in popularity in recent years along with the trend toward a desire for higher arrow speed.

which translates to the higher velocity that most archers seek today. However, the composite shafts typically share similar production problems with fiberglass and are considerably more expensive. Regardless, a bowhunter seeking to improve arrow trajectory by reducing the physical weight of his shafts might find the answer in graphite. Graphite is comparatively durable. When stressed, graphite shafts do not bend out of shape, but they can break.

Shaft Cosmetics

In recent years more and more arrows have become available in commercial camouflage patterns. This is less a functional feature and more a case of arrow manufacturers jockeying for a bigger share of the market by appealing to certain consumers. Camo shafts may be an advantage in some cases, however, such as when hunting keen-eyed game like turkeys. Your choice of shaft color is strictly a matter of personal preference. Many bowhunters use the less-expensive solid color shafts for target shooting and plinking, and switch to camo shafts when they go hunting.

Many arrows are also dipped or crested for aesthetic, practical, or personal reasons; however, applications of paint or lacquer is generally an optional choice.

Shaft Length

Your arrow length is determined by nocking an uncut arrow and drawing it, naturally and comfortably, into shooting posi-

Photo by Karl Gunzer Jr.

Measure proper shaft length by drawing an uncut shaft on the bow you plan to shoot, and having an assistant mark the draw length even with the back of your bow, plus another half to three-quarters of an inch to ensure good broadhead clearance.

tion. A felt-tip pen or pencil may be used to mark the shaft where it is even with the back of your bow (the side farthest away from you). By adding an additional half- to three-quarters of an inch to this mark, you'll have the draw length you need for your hunting arrows. The extra length is needed for adequate broadhead clearance. Arrows used in overdraw bows are typically shorter than standard hunting shafts. Also, compound bow shooters normally have a slightly longer draw length than recurve or longbow shooters.

You want matched hunting arrows suited to you and your bow. Settle for nothing less. Consistent accuracy is impossible unless the arrows are straight, uniformly spined, and of identical weight.

Arrow Points

Arrow points are designed for either practice or hunting. Steel practice points are available in weights identical to hunting heads and may be used where practice with broadheads is not practical. A blunt of steel or hard rubber is designed for use on small game. Steel broadheads are used in bowhunting and come in a variety of weights, shapes, and blade configurations.

All points are attached to the shaft by screw-in adaptors or by a hot-melt cement. Points must be aligned properly to ensure correct arrow flight.

Broadheads

Broadheads are of most importance to archers from a bowhunting standpoint. All broadheads have three basic components: the tip, the blades, and the ferrule, or body of the head.

There are two basic types of broadheads: fixed-blade and modular with replaceable blades. Whichever the bowhunter's choice, quality heads share certain characteristics. They fly accurately, penetrate deeply, and cut cleanly.

Broadhead Flight

While some bowhunters complain about difficulty in getting arrows to fly straight with broadheads, there is no great mystery to attaining accuracy with hunting heads. Virtually all modern broadheads are precision-machined and thus straight and well-balanced from the factory. A hunter with broadheads of the correct weight for the spine of his arrow, mounted correctly and tuned, should have no trouble getting good arrow flight. This will be discussed further in the shooting section.

**Broadheads are generally categorized by their number of blades
and point style. Most have three or four blades and have a sharpened
point, chisel point, pencil point or an unorthodox type of tip.**

Photo by Karl Gunzer Jr.

Be sure to test-shoot various broadheads to find out which type flies best from your bow. A block of styrofoam or ethafoam makes a good backstop for broadheads.

Sharpness

Since arrows lack the shocking power of bullets, they must kill by creating a great amount of bleeding. Unless broadheads truly are shaving-sharp, they should never be used for hunting. This point cannot be overstated. No responsible bowhunter would ever shoot dull broadheads at game. Arrow-hit animals rarely fall within sight of the shooter and an ample blood trail aids in quick recovery of bowhunting trophies.

Attaining sharpness can be a problem with fixed-blade heads unless the bowhunter has knowledge of sharpening methods or access to sharpening devices. Quality replacement blades come from the factory presharpened, an advantage for some hunters.

Despite claims of manufacturers, not all of these heads with factory-sharpened blades are suitable for hunting until honed to scalpel sharpness. And despite what some shooters believe, interchangeable blades may be—and often should be—resharpened. Some bowhunters use practice-dulled blades until ready to hunt, at which time they simply replace them with unused, shaving-sharp blades. Others touch up the practice heads and use them for hunting.

Bow weight, arrow weight, trueness of arrow flight, and position or movement of the target all affect penetration.

Photo by Mike Strandlund

Broadheads must be razor sharp. A good test for sharpness is running the edge across a stretched rubber band, which closely matches the resilience of a blood vessel. An edge that's sharp enough will cut the rubber band, while a dull one won't.

Once an arrow is released, what follows is beyond the shooter's control. This underscores the need to use only broadheads that are absolutely sharp. Marginal and even poor hits may prove fatal if sufficient hemorrhage results. Dull heads do not kill efficiently and should never be used in bowhunting.

It is important to understand that any broadhead can become dull over a period of time, even if it has not been used. Bowhunters need to check broadhead sharpness regularly, especially if the arrows are carried in a quiver and occasionally removed and reinserted. Some hunters apply a thin coat of machine oil or petroleum jelly to the cutting edges of their broadheads. Such a protective coating can prevent rust; however, moderation is encouraged.

Penetration

Equally important to good accuracy is good penetration. Without sufficient penetration, a perfect shot may be ineffective.

A broadhead's ability to penetrate is determined by how

much friction it creates. A smaller broadhead with a sharp tip and sharp blades penetrates with a minimum of friction. All things being equal, it will penetrate deeper than a head with a large surface area or components that "push" through the animal, rather than cut their way through.

Unfortunately, all shots on game are not equal, and that has led to a controversy over what is the best design of broadhead. Fixed-blade broadheads generally penetrate better through hide, large muscles and organs, because their razor tips begin cutting immediately on impact; the entire blade is razor-sharp and will thus cut best.

However, penetration through soft tissue is usually not an issue with modern archery gear. A sharp broadhead on an arrow propelled from an average bow will pass cleanly through most big game if it encounters only soft tissue. Most penetration problems arise when the broadhead encounters bone. Vertebrae, leg bones, and shoulder blades can stop arrows from making the kill. For dealing with these bony obstructions, many bowhunters depend on chisel-tipped broadheads. A strong chisel tip will split some bones that would stop or bend sharp-to-the-point heads. With less energy spent and the tip intact, the chisel-point will usually have better penetration after striking the bone. Along with this ability to handle bone, the chisel point also has three or four sharp edges that cut to a certain degree, though the blades do most of that work.

A third type of broadhead tip is the pointed conical, or pencil point. This type is rapidly losing popularity as bowhunters realize that the pointed conical has neither cutting ability of the sharp-to-the-tip fixed-blade broadhead nor the bone-splitting/cutting ability of the chisel.

Which penetrates better, a blade with two, three, four or more blades? There are many variables involved. A two-blade head has less blade friction, and on certain shots the blades may slip between bones whereas a head with more blades would lodge between the bones. However, the two blades cut only a slot, rather than a hole, and the ferrule thus encounters more friction. A three-blade head cuts a hole, but has the added friction of another blade. A four-blade head has still another blade to create friction, while those heads with six and eight blades not only have proportionally greater friction, but the multiple blades impede each other's cutting ability.

Another factor affecting penetration is construction. Nothing hurts penetration more than broken blades. Some broadheads have blades that are thicker and otherwise more resistant to breakage than others. Others come from the factory with blades that are too dull for hunting.

Broadhead companies and archery experts have done hundreds of tests designed to rate penetration of various broadheads. Each test has different variables and each gives different conclusions on which style of head is best. Whatever broadhead you choose to hunt with, make sure it will fly straight from your bow and the blades are razor-sharp and high quality.

Cutting Diameter

Some people believe that a bigger hole or more blades, which cut more, is more important than penetration. A larger cutting diameter may help in some cases; for example, larger blades or additional blades will cut more capillaries and may reach more major vessels than a smaller head would. But a hunter should never seek a larger hole as a tradeoff to penetration. Two holes—primarily an exit hole—is most important in leaving a good blood trail, which is often necessary for recovering the animal.

Broadhead Function and Features

Some fixed-blade broadheads have earned a reputation for being noisy and difficult to control. Blade design may cause a few heads to whistle as air passes through the vents; however, this is rarely a problem today. More likely is some sort of flight-control difficulty, especially with larger broadheads. A possible remedy is to increase the arrow's spine or change the size and shape of the fletching. A final option if problems persist is to choose another broadhead.

Both fixed-blade and replacement-type broadheads come in various weights, sizes, and shapes. Most do the job for which they were created; however, there are some general rules to consider when searching for the ideal broadhead:

- Solid one-piece heads are tougher than broadheads with blades designed to be replaced after every shot. Replacement-type heads should have a locking system that holds the blades securely in place.
- Heads made of carbon steel are easier to sharpen but are affected by moisture and can rust. Stainless steel broadheads are impervious to wet weather and humidity.
- Most broadheads have a cutting width of one to 1 ½

inches. Length varies, but longer heads are usually made thicker to strengthen the point. Note that must states have laws regulating dimensions as well as style of broadheads.

- Heads with serrated blades are more difficult to sharpen and keep sharp than broadheads with smooth edges. Hair, fat, and tissue can collect in serrations and impede penetration and blood flow.

- Heads with movable blades that spread on contact and cut in a scissoring fashion generally do not penetrate well. Those currently in production have large, pencil-point tips that do not pierce well, and their mechanisms absorb energy that would otherwise be used for deeper penetration.

- Broadheads often fly differently than field or target points of the same weight. Heads should be test-shot carefully to determine their accuracy. Resharpen or replace blades before hunting.

- Broadheads typically weigh between 125 and 145 grains, but lighter and heavier heads are available. Match the weight of practice points and broadheads.

- Broadhead alignment is vital for accuracy. To check mounted heads, stand the arrow on its point and spin the shaft like a top. If a wobble is apparent where the shaft and broadhead meet, replace or straighten the head.

- Misaligned broadheads may be the result of bent tips or improper mounting. Bent heads may be straightened or discarded. It may be necessary to loosen the broadhead from its adaptor or, in the case of tapered wood shafts or swagged metal shafts with a normal five-degree taper, to remove

Photo by Karl Gunzer Jr.

Spin broadheads on a smooth surface to check for straightness. There should be no wobble where the head meets the shaft.

the head itself. Hot-melt glue is handy for this corrective procedure. Heating the arrow shaft insert allows loosening or removal of the head, which may be spin-tested and adjusted until it no longer wobbles.

- Broadhead problems show up more on light, fast-flying arrows, where proper alignment is especially critical. Slower, heavier arrows are more forgiving. Correctly mounted broadheads should be a goal of all bowhunters no matter their choice of equipment.

Only by shopping around, test-shooting different heads, and judging performance will you be able to settle on what's best for you. The best advice is shoot any head you like as long as it's strong, razor-sharp, and flies well from your hunting bow.

Other Arrow Points

Other arrow points of interest to the hunter are field tips, blunts, Judo points, and bird points.

The field point is a large target-shooting point. Hunters practice with field points of the same weight as the broadheads they plan to use after they get broadheads and field points to fly the same by tuning their bows (see Chapter 5). Never use field points for hunting, even small game, because they lack the cutting ability of broadheads and shocking power of the other points.

Photo by Karl Gunzer Jr.

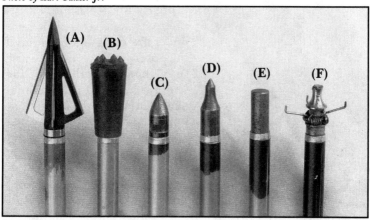

Screw-in adaptors allow archers to change arrow points to suit their needs. Broadheads (A) are used for big game hunting. Rubber blunts (B) can be used for some small game. Bullet and field points (C and D) are best suited for target practice. Metal blunts and Judo points (E and F) are good for small game hunting and stump shooting.

37

Blunts, Judos and bird points are used for hunting small game. They kill by shock. Each is designed to deliver all the arrow's energy to the game by striking with little or no penetration. The blunt is a large, rounded steel or rubber point. Judo is a trademark for a large field tip with spring arms that can be used for small game, though it is best suited for "stump shooting," because the springs keep arrows from becoming lost. The bird point is a blunt with large, stiff wires that make it easier to hit a moving target.

A fish point has barbs instead of blades that keep carp, suckers, and other species commonly sought by bowfishermen from pulling off. There are many designs of fish points. First-rate features include barbs that resist planing in water, hold the fish well, and are easily removed or turned around to help you remove the arrow from the fish.

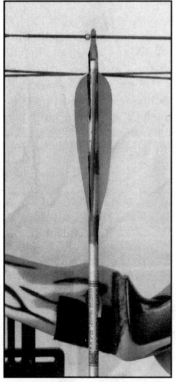

Photo by Karl Gunzer Jr.

Most bowhunters use nocks that snap on the string to keep the arrow securely in place while drawing and shooting. The nock should not grip too tightly, however, or accuracy will suffer.

Nocks

Nocks are typically made of plastic and fit on the same end of the arrows as the fletching. The nocks are grooved to fit the bowstring and must be aligned properly for consistently accurate arrow flight. Different nocks are designed for special purposes. Many archers use snap-on nocks made to grip the string snugly and prevent accidental unnocking. Conversely, some use smooth, soft-plastic nocks designed for minimal resistance on the string at the release.

Two features in nocks to consider are visibility and indexing. Some hunters use fluorescent nocks that catch light and let them see where their arrow is traveling. You might also want a nock with an index, or a small bump on one side that allows you to correctly nock an arrow by feel, which can save time and movement.

Fletching

Fletching—the "rudder" at the back end of the arrow—is designed to help control the arrow in flight by controlling air flow and resistance. It is either pliable plastic material, called vanes, or wing feathers from wild or domestic turkeys. The three or four vanes or feathers are attached to the shaft in a straight, offset, or helical (spiral) configuration.

The type of fletching you choose depends on the type of performance you seek from your arrow. Large, helical fletching imparts spin and wind resistance to the arrow, which gives the most stability to the arrow but slows it down. Smaller, lighter, straight fletching improves speed but stability may be lost. Plastic vanes are more durable and are less affected by rain than feathers. Feathers have the advantage of being lighter than plastic, which enhances arrow velocity, and they "give" as the arrow launches past the handle riser, lessening the chance the arrow will be bumped off course.

Most bowhunting fletching is five inches long and mounted helically to stabilize and control the flight of a broadhead-tipped arrow. Most hunting arrows have three vanes or feathers, two of one color (hen feathers) and one of another color (cock

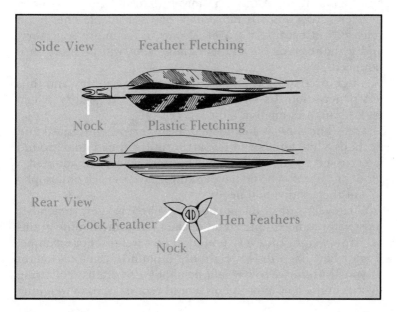

feather). The cock feather is usually at a right angle to the bowstring, away from the bow, when the arrow is nocked. Some bowhunters prefer four-fletched hunting arrows, which may be nocked and shot quickly without the shooter paying attention to the position of the fletching.

Arrow Selection

Your final choice of arrow and hunting head will depend on several objective and subjective judgments. You may, for example, opt to shoot aluminum because of its availability and versatility. You may decide on feathers rather than vanes not because of any minor functional difference, but simply because you prefer the look and feel of feathers. You may select a replaceable-blade broadhead because you never had much luck getting a good edge on fixed-blade heads.

Arrow Weight

One important decision you'll have to make is whether to use arrows that are light, medium-weight or heavy. Any bow can handle a wide range of arrow weights as long as weight, spine and fletching are correctly matched to provide good arrow flight. Each weight level has its own advantages and disadvantages.

All other things being equal, a heavier arrow will have the best penetration. Although slower than a lighter arrow, a heavier arrow absorbs more of a bow's available energy on release. But because it travels slower, it has more trajectory, and a slight error on a longer-range shot will be more pronounced.

A lighter arrow has greater speed but less energy and thus less penetration. Its faster flight means less trajectory, which makes range estimation a bit less critical.

And while there is a handful of heavy arrow enthusiasts and perhaps a like number of fast arrow buffs, the middle ground is occupied by an army of bowhunters who have adopted a moderate approach and have adapted parts of each philosophy to suit their individual needs.

Whatever your ultimate choice of arrow weight, remember most veteran bowhunters and dealers recommend nine grains of arrow weight for every pound of bow weight. For example, if your bow has a draw weight of 55 pounds, the total weight of your hunting arrow would be about 495 grains. Following this formula, a 60-pound bow would require arrows weighing

540 grains; a 65-pound bow needs 585-grain arrows, and so on. Minor variations in this bow/arrow weight ratio are acceptable and common. Unfortunately, when you drastically reduce arrow weight in a quest for speed, you're using arrows that cannot absorb as much of the bow's energy as normal arrows. Excess energy is dissipated in noisy vibrations that can shorten your bow's life.

Other Considerations

Your bow's draw weight and your personal draw length are important considerations in arrow selection. As noted in the last chapter, correct bow weight depends on such factors as strength and the game animal being hunted. Your bow's poundage determines the spine—or stiffness—of the shafts you'll shoot.

Another important consideration may be price. If you're like most bowhunters, you watch your pennies and do what you can to get the most from each dollar you spend. Some arrows and heads are quite costly; others are suspiciously inexpensive. Your ultimate decision may well be influenced by your checkbook balance or your credit card status. Regardless, good arrows and good broadheads can last for several seasons if cared for properly, while bowhunters often pay dearly for inexpensive, poor-quality shafts and heads because they must be replaced often.

CHAPTER 3
BOWHUNTING ACCESSORIES

Time was when a bowhunter's basic gear consisted of a stout bow, matched arrows, and carefully honed hunting heads. Throw in an armguard and shooting glove, add a quiver to carry extra arrows, and you had all you needed. Although it's generally agreed this basic gear is all anyone

Photo by Mike Strandlund

Most bowhunters today would feel lost without the array of gear that aids them in hunting and shooting. Bringing along the right equipment, and leaving the junk at home, will help you be a better bowhunter.

really needs to bowhunt, today's bowhunter seldom limits himself to these basics. Visit an archery shop or scan the pages of a bowhunting catalog and you will find a wide–and often confusing–array of equipment.

So how do you determine what's right for you? A good way to begin is to ask yourself questions and give honest answers. For example, do you hunt mainly from trees? If so, a tree stand, steps, haul line, and safety belt should appear on your accessories list. On the other hand, if most of your time is spent still-hunting, you may want to list a pair of binoculars and sturdy but quiet footwear near the top of your list. Really, only you can determine what's essential for your particular hunting style, method, and locale. In time you'll learn to separate practical items from nonessentials.

Shooting Gear

Most archers have a few standard accessories that they take to the field with them on every outing. These items, such as quivers, armguards, and a shooting glove or tab help maintain consistent shooting. No matter what equipment you choose, practice with it before the season to be sure it fits your needs.

Quivers

Three basic types of quivers in use today are bow quivers, back quivers, and belt or hip quivers. Each type has advantages and drawbacks.

Courtesy Chuck Adams

Most hunters favor multi-arrow quivers that attach directly to their bow. These quivers are relatively sturdy and hold the arrows

Photo Courtesy Delta Industries

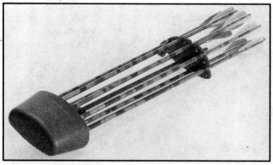

Quivers that attach to the bow or the belt are most widely used today, though a few hunters still opt for quivers slung across the back.

in position for a quick second shot. While they are convenient, they do add extra weight to one side of the bow, and shooting accuracy may be slightly affected as the weight of the bow changes each time another arrow is plucked from the quiver. Bow quivers also make shooting in higher winds more difficult, as the added surface area of the quiver and complement of arrows catch the wind. These drawbacks considered, the bow quiver remains the most popular.

Some hunters opt for hooded back quivers which are worn like backpacks. These quivers generally hold a lot of arrows and some have a small compartment that acts as a daypack. While some like these quivers, they can be inconvenient if the archer likes to sit often, or carry a lot of gear. Some archers insist on wearing shoulder quivers; however, these quivers allow arrows to rattle noisily as the wearer walks and may be dangerous in the event of a fall.

A few archers choose belt quivers that fit on the hip. These are generally most convenient in open areas where you don't have to slip through thick cover or briars. They keep arrows handy at the side, weight off the bow, and allow you to wear a backpack.

Your choice of quiver is strictly a matter of personal preference, but be sure it has a hood that completely covers the razor-sharp broadheads. Rubber grippers that hold each individual shaft securely and quietly in the quiver are used by most bowhunters. Also, make sure the quiver is convenient and allows removal of an arrow with a minimum of movement and noise.

Armguards

An armguard serves two basic purposes. First, it prevents painful bruises caused by the bowstring slapping the inside of the bow arm. Second, it holds bulky or baggy sleeves out of the way as the arrow is released. A bowstring that snags on clothing will cause the arrow to fly erratically. Hunting armguards should be comfortable, weatherproof, and quiet.

A bowhunter's need for an armguard is determined by his shooting style, the bow used, and the clothing worn. Some archers have no need for an armguard, while others need a long armguard that protects the inside of the entire arm. In extreme cold it may be necessary to use a chest protector, which keeps bulky clothing out of the path of the bowstring. Practice in your hunting clothes to determine your needs.

An armguard and finger tab or glove are standard equipment for bowhunters, protecting them from bowstring abrasions.

Shooting Gloves/Tabs

The shooting fingers should be protected from abrasion by the bowstring and allow for a clean, quick release. Leather shooting gloves encase and protect the three fingers of the shooting hand individually, and are held in place by a wrist strap.

Tabs, usually made of leather, felt or calf hair, are durable, inexpensive, and allow for a smooth release. They are held in place by a loop that slips over the middle finger.

Mechanical Release Aids

In the past virtually all bowhunters "shot with fingers" and regarded the glove or tab as a vital part of their gear. The feel of the bowstring and simplicity of use still appeals to the majority of bowhunters. Archers seeking a better release, and improved arrow flight, speed, and accuracy, often use a mechanical release. While these benefits may be great, a release is not as dependable as fingers, and has the possibility of fouling with ice or debris and costing the bowhunter a shooting opportunity; losing or breaking one can ruin a hunt. Most bowhunters who use a release carry a spare with them in the field. Once a bow is sighted in with a release, it rarely shoots in the same spot when fired with fingers.

Photo by Karl Gunzer Jr.

Bowstring release aids can help an archer get a smoother, crisper release, but there are some disadvantages in using these devices for bowhunting.

There are many models of mechanical releases. Some attach to the shooter's wrist, while others are held in the palm of the hand (concho models), or grasped by the fingers (T-shaped models). Releases are attached to the bowstring by metal pins or nylon cords, some held vertically and others horizontally. Triggering is done by depressing a button, squeezing a trigger, or releasing a trigger that has been cocked by squeezing. They are illegal in some areas.

Bow Stringers

Early-day bowhunters commonly braced their bows by using the step-through or push-pull stringing method, using their bodies to bend and string their bows. The former could twist and damage the bow's limbs; the latter caused numerous injuries–including blindness in a few cases–when the hand or bow tip slipped. The safest, most efficient method of stringing a recurve or longbow is to use a bow stringer. Stringers are usually cords with leather pockets at each end for the bow tips. To string the bow once the stringer is in place, you simply step on the bow stringer and lift up on the bow while slipping the bowstring loop into place on the bow's upper limb.

Several types of bow stringers are available for compound bows. However, they are seldom needed thanks to the development of cables with teardrop string attachments. These allow new strings to be easily fitted without first removing the old bowstring.

Bow Cases

Bow cases are designed to prevent damage during transport and come in hard and soft models. Hard cases of wood, plastic, or aluminum are ideal for travel by air or vehicle. Most are large enough to carry a hunting bow as well as a dozen or more arrows, a quiver, and miscellaneous tackle.

Soft cases of cloth and suitable padding are best used on short hauls between home and hunting or practice areas. A few have pockets for accessory items and some are big enough to include protection for a bow quiver and its complement of arrows.

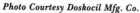

Photo Courtesy Doskocil Mfg. Co.

A bow case can be your most important piece of equipment on a trip, protecting bow and arrows from damage that could cause a malfunction or missed shot.

Tackle Box

Most serious bowhunters keep a small tackle box handy. Tools such as pliers, screwdrivers, and Allen wrenches are often included along with extra broadheads, nocks, epoxy or ferrule cement, adapters, broadhead wrench, bow square, nocking points, arrow rests, tape, bowstring wax, fletching glue, sight pins, spare batteries, arrow puller, spare bowstring, and anything else that may be needed. While you won't need all this in the field with you, it pays to have it back at camp or in your vehicle should you encounter difficulties during your hunt.

Bowhunting Accessories

While the equipment you hunt with will remain fairly constant from one outing to the next, the method of hunting and the quarry pursued will necessitate different accessories. Will you be hunting from the ground or a tree? Does the animal have a keen sense of smell? Are you hunting in thick cover or open plains? All these questions affect the proper gear for your bag.

Photo by Mike Strandlund

A tackle box with spare parts and tools can save the day if you have any equipment problems.

Photo by Richard P. Smith

String trackers that attach from the bow to the arrow make for easy tracking under poor conditions.

Photo by Mike Strandlund

A fanny pack or backpack filled with the right gear can make your hunt safer, more enjoyable, and more productive.

Day Packs and Supplies

Many bowhunters wear a pack of some sort each time they venture afield. These may range from small fanny packs to elaborate backpacks. A person hunting a midwestern woodlot may opt to wear a fanny pack containing his lunch, rain slicker, flashlight, and a nylon rope. Another, roaming the Rocky Mountain high country, may need a backpack with survival gear, including a first-aid kit and signaling devices, along with routine equipment. Only the individual hunter can decide what's needed and what's needless weight. There are those who would not hunt *anywhere* without such items as a compass, waterproof matches, signal whistle, food, a canteen, cord, and space blanket. An emergency can occur at any time, and the admonition to be prepared applies no less to bowhunters than to Boy Scouts.

Certain gear such as insect repellent, game scents, toilet paper, a pencil or pen, flashlight, matches or lighter and a compass fit well into pockets. Yet packs and the extra room they provide are certainly worth consideration by any bowhunter.

Packs should be quiet and water resistant. Branches scratching a nylon pack will spook game, and spare clothes or gear may be useless if your pack gets wet. Polar fleece and wool are better pack shell materials. The few extra dollars spent on a quality product will be worthwhile in comfort and durability.

Cutting Devices

Carrying a knife afield is based more on common sense than optimism. A good folding or sheath knife is mandatory, not only for dressing game but for doing dozens of other jobs.

Knives come in an endless variety of sizes and designs, each best for certain purposes. Anticipate your needs and select the knife accordingly. If you opt for a folding knife, make sure it has a sturdy locking device that will not let it snap closed. A sharpening stone or hone may be needed.

A small folding saw, capable of fitting in a pocket or pack, is handy for certain field-dressing jobs and for clearing shooting lanes. On an extended trip, a machete or axe may be helpful.

Portable Tree Stands and Steps

Portable tree stands allow hunters to choose different locations to suit wind conditions and travel patterns–two keys to successful bowhunting. Consequently, portable tree stands are a must item on the equipment list of many bowhunters. Many bowhunters have a network of stands, choosing the best stand depending on weather conditions, time of day, and hunting pressure. Many types of stands are available, including ladder stands, climbing stands, and hang-on models.

Ladder stands work well on small trees that may have trouble supporting your weight. They are sturdy, but their weight and bulk make them difficult to carry for long distances or through thick cover. Many climbing stands are lightweight and popular with hunters who like to change locations often, but may be

Photos by Mike Strandlund

A tree stand and steps are standard equipment for most bowhunters today, especially whitetail hunters.

Photo by Mike Strandlund

Any time you hunt out of a tree, use a safety belt. Falls from trees are a leading cause of hunter injury.

noisy while climbing, and cannot be used on all trees. Chain-on stands take time to set up, but are sturdy and can be left on the tree for a period of time.

Unless you have a climbing tree stand or ladder model, you'll need a separate means of getting into the tree. Belt-on or screw-in steps are among your options. A few bowhunters scale trees with the aid of a ladder or strap-on climbing device similar to those worn by telephone linemen. You may bolt or nail wood blocks to a tree trunk if you have permission or own the trees. You may use heavy gauge wire or rope to attach the blocks if you don't. If you use portable steps, it's a good idea to take them with you when you leave the woods.

Some of the most disabling hunting injuries today involve falls from tree stands. If you use a tree stand, *always* wear a safety belt, and put it on before you get in the stand. Use a haul line to bring up any gear. Many tree stand accessories are available, including bow hangers, arrow holders, seat cushions, blinds and even umbrellas. Use whatever it takes to be comfortable without overburdening yourself with gadgets.

Calls, Scents and Decoys

Depending on what you are hunting, bringing the animal to you may provide your best chance for bagging game. Game calls, scents, and decoys are the tools of the trade.

Scent is often the bowhunter's worst enemy, but in the right circumstances may lead to success. Cover scents are designed to mask human odors so animals are not alerted to your presence. Attractors, including sex scents and food scents, are used to help bring in your quarry and position it for a killing shot. While nothing is sure-fire, many hunters tell success stories that credit good use of scents.

Game calling has applications from squirrels and turkeys to elk or moose. In the right situation any animal will respond

Photo Courtesy Robbins Scents

Photo by Karl Gunzer Jr.

Attracting game by use of calls and scent can put excitement into your hunt. Sales of these is big business and a hunter must choose quailty products.

to a call. Whether rattling in whitetails, calling coyotes, or bugling elk, the keys are practice and patience. Just remember, any animal coming to the call is alert and looking for whatever made that sound. You may therefore be spotted while drawing, or the animal may "jump the string" at the sound of the shot.

Decoys help to draw game into effective range and focus the animal's attention away from the hunter, possibly making it easier to draw your bow.

Experiment with different calls, scents and decoys depending on what and where you're hunting. Keep in mind that calls and decoys may attract other hunters as well as the game you are after, presenting additional safety concerns.

Optics

Binoculars and spotting scopes are used by an increasing number of serious bowhunters. Good optics can pay dividends for any bowhunter, no matter where or how you hunt or what species you pursue. Lightweight, compact binoculars are easy to carry into the field, though full-size binoculars usually have better resolution and are easier to use for extended periods of glassing. Powerful spotting scopes are beneficial for open-country hunting. Quality, usually proportional to price, should be the watchword when selecting hunting optics.

Optical rangefinders are used by some bowhunters to help determine yardage accurately. These devices commonly work by creating two images that merge when the proper yardage is dialed. Rangefinders should be seriously considered for hunting open areas where longer shot opportunities are common, especially if you are in unfamiliar terrain.

Bowhunters who wear glasses or contact lenses should always have a spare pair in their pack, vehicle or at camp. Breaking or losing your only pair of corrective lenses will ruin your hunting trip.

Other Gear

Some basic gear should be carried on every hunt, depending on where and what you're hunting. Any time you may be in the woods after dark, carry a **flashlight**. It identifies you as a person to others, and will help you in find your way or follow a blood trail. If you hunt in a state where it is illegal to move an animal without first completing your tag, carry a **pen** or pencil with your license.

Photo by Mike Strandlund

Optics—binoculars and spotting scopes—can help you find game, judge antlers, and save time and energy.

If you're in an area where there is a possibility of getting lost, carry a **compass** and know how to use it. Invest in a good quality, liquid-filled compass with a luminescent dial. Many types are available, including those you carry in your pocket, pin to your coat, or strap on your wrist.

Equally important are **maps** of your hunting area. They not only help you stay found, but can be used to help locate new hunting areas and game. Topographical maps can be ordered by contacting: Branch of Distribution, U.S. Geological Survey, Box 25286, Denver, CO 80225; telephone 303/236-7477. Maps cost $2.50, which covers postage. Indexes to identify the maps you need may be ordered free of charge.

Aside from its normal use, **toilet paper** can be handy for marking a blood trail. **Plastic bags** can be used for keeping animal parts such as the liver and heart, and **plastic gloves** can protect you from disease and make clean-up easy. If you're hunting in country where two hands may be required for treacherous travel, invest in a **bow sling**, which allows you to hang your bow from your shoulder.

If you're hunting from a stand location, thumbtacks with

reflective tape on the end are useful for finding your way to and from your stand in the dark, and can easily be removed at the end of the season. To help you keep ready, **bow holders** that attach to your belt and tie to your leg relieve the strain on your bow arm from holding a heavy bow. **Arrow holders** which attach to the bow and grip the arrow help keep your arrow from falling from the rest should you cant your bow or bump your arrow. When you begin your draw, the arrow holder releases its grip. Household **string** or cord have a multitude of uses, and should be a standard item in your pack.

Clothing

Available in a variety of patterns and materials, camouflage pants, shirts, jackets, hats, and accessories are the standard dress of today's bowhunter.

Photo by Gerald A. Almy

The close-range, deliberate nature of bowhunting generally eliminates the need for hunter orange and dictates the use of clothing that helps hide the hunter. If you choose to bowhunt during regular firearms seasons, blaze orange should be worn for safety, and may be required by law.

Outerwear

Quiet, durable, comfortable and practical, good camo clothing can be a bowhunter's best friend and increase your chances for success. Camouflage should match your surroundings. Dull colors with mottled patterns are ideal for blending into shadows. Tree bark patterns are obviously best if you take a stand against a large tree, and are a good

A properly dressed bowhunter should have clothes that provide the right amount of warmth, quietness, and shade for the eyes.

55

choice for many other situations. While a treestand hunter may use a bark pattern effectively, his surroundings, from a deer's perspective, will be dominated by sky and branches. In this case a light-colored camo pattern is often best, though on a very overcast day a bark pattern may blend best with the trees and the sky.

Some hunting garments on the market look like good camo on the rack, but are not very functional in the woods. In some cases there isn't enough contrast to break up the hunter's outline; in other cases the lighter tones are too light and make movement easy for the game to spot. Pay close attention to patterns and tones of your camouflage; they could determine the outcome of your hunt.

When buying a hunting outfit, bowhunters have to keep several things in mind. If still-hunting and stalking will be the main approach, quietness is most important. Cotton, wool, or fleecetype outerwear is best. Synthetic materials like nylon are too noisy.

In rainy weather, and especially on extended hunts, high-quality rainwear is important. It, too, should be camouflaged, and quiet and dull-colored when wet. If the hunt will be in cold weather, camo outerwear must be roomy enough for warm undergarments. The top must not fit too loosely, however, or it may interfere with the bowstring. Most hunters prefer to dress in layers, which allows them to adjust their insulation as the weather changes.

Some research has shown that animals may perceive ultraviolet light better than humans, and concern has arisen over the amount of phosphates used in laundry detergents since they may cause clothes to "glow" in low light conditions. Many bowhunters wash their hunting clothes in basic detergents that contain no phosphates and no scents. Several types of hunter's clothes detergents are available.

Underwear

An often overlooked source of warmth and comfort is good quality underwear. To remain warm without adding overly bulky clothes, invest in quality underwear such as polypropylene or Thermax. These types of underwear are more durable than traditional cotton, and have wicking properties that draw moisture away from your skin. This is important if you are active, or the temperature in your hunting area fluctuates a great deal.

Hats and Caps

A hat or cap performs many functions for the bowhunter. It keeps your head warm with insulation or cool with shade. It provides camouflage with its color and shades the face from rain, snow and sun. A hat may even help contain the hunter's scent by covering the hair–a major producer of human scent.

A bowhunter may have a need for several types of hats, even in a single outing, and should have at least a couple types along on each hunting trip. Stiff-brimmed caps may interfere with the bowstring, throwing off the shot or knocking off the cap. Few hunters can use a baseball-cap style worn in the usual fashion; some wear these caps askew with the brim to the side or back. A better choice is the Jones style hat or the jungle guerilla type with a floppy, adjustable brim that can be customized to the situation. In colder weather, wool stocking caps are an ideal choice.

Photos by Mike Strandlund

Footwear

Your footwear should be matched to the weather, terrain, and tactics you are using. In most instances they must be waterproof. In most cases, rubber boots are the first choice for bowhunters. They diminish the scent a you leave on the way to your stand, and reduce the amount of odor your feet release while there. Rubber is also waterproof and inexpensive.

If you hunt rugged terrain, you'll need leather boots with good traction and support. For cold weather or stand hunting, insulated pacs are usually the best choice for

Rubber soled boots are often the best choice for bowhunters as they are waterproof and leave little human scent behind. Rugged terrain and cold weather may require leather boots with vibram soles and good ankle support.

comfort. Depending on weather and terrain, the best boots may be rubber hip boots, or even tennis shoes. Consider your footwear carefully–it can affect your hunting enjoyment and success.

Camo Accessories

Unless camouflage is extended to include a hunter's face and hands–as well as his equipment–the attempts at concealment are incomplete. Most big game animals seem to spot a human face readily. More and more bowhunters use camouflage face paint or headnets to keep from being spotted.

If you use paint, cover your neck and ears as well as your face. The best headnets give full-face coverage, as long as looking through the mesh does not hamper your eyesight. You may also use a handkerchief tied around your face or, in cold weather, a ski mask.

Deer and other big game animals are most adept at spotting movement, which means your hands must also be camouflaged. Either paint or gloves will work. Some hunters cut off some fingers of their gloves to accommodate a shooting glove or tab.

Any equipment such as your bow, quiver, backpack, and tree stand should also be camouflaged with paint, tape, or natural camouflage.

Woodsmanship and Travel Gear

Bowhunting often unites hunters as they venture into new areas to pursue game. If you're planning a trip, get together with your companions several months ahead of time and plan what gear you will need and who will bring it. Be sure that every member has maps of the location, along with a good quality compass. Go over the hunting areas and plan your hunt. Be sure everyone has the proper hunting licenses, tags, stamps, and written permission slips where required.

Other gear may be necessary if you are planning an extended hunt.

Camping Equipment

On an extended hunting trip, you'll need camping equipment. The easiest way to camp is with a travel trailer or pickup camper. Your camp is self-contained, and you won't need to worry too much about the weather. Unfortunately most hunters aren't afforded the luxury of hard-sided units and resort to tenting.

Tents come in a variety of designs, each for a different purpose. Most popular today is the three-man dome tent with a removable rain fly. It is a good compromise in weight, price, and roominess. For long stays, however, you'll appreciate the extra space provided by a larger dome or wall tent.

Very small tents are seldom worth buying, with one exception. There are high-quality, lightweight tents that can be carried routinely in a daypack. If you are hunting far away from camp and spot game in the evening, you can pull out your tent, set up a spike camp and be waiting at first light.

Large, canvas wall tents are often used in remote country hunts where you'll spend a week or more in the field. Some

Photo by Mike Strandlund

Photo by Gerald A. Almy

Camping trips vary from an overnight in a tent to an elaborate back-country set-up. Be sure to pack equipment accordingly.

stores and outfitters will rent you tents if you're a do-it-yourself-er, but be sure to arrange for good transportation–big tents are heavy. Your tent should have a floor. If not, use a tarp or piece of plastic to help keep you and your gear free of dirt.

If you're camping in cold country, a heater will be a nice addition. Among your options are wood stoves, kerosene stoves, and catalytic heaters. Wood and kerosene are the warmest options, but take up a lot of space. Catalytic heaters are not as effective if its bitterly cold, but are smaller and more convenient. Whatever type of heating you use, be sure there's adequate ventilation to avoid asphyxiation.

Some kind of lighting around camp is a necessity. Flashlights are good for small chores, but you should have a central unit that provides illumination. Lanterns are the norm, fueled by propane, white gas, or even regular gasoline. Be sure to have plenty of fuel, matches and extra mantles.

Sleeping gear

When camping, the standard choice for bedding is a quality sleeping bag. Blankets and pillows may be warm enough in a motel or camper, but are unwieldy to pack along on trips and provide substandard warmth.

Down bags are expensive but will keep you warm in bitter cold. Be aware, however, that there are various grades of down. Some sleeping bags are filled with feathers, or have only a percentage of down. Goose down is the premier filler, and the most expensive. The label on the bag should identify the kind of down and how many ounces are in the bag. If you choose a down bag, be sure to keep it dry. Down bags are cold and clammy if wet, and will take forever to dry.

Synthetic fillers, on the other hand, are easily dried and will retain heat when wet because they retain their loft. Most are not as expensive as down, but some will keep you just as warm. Generally they are a little heavier, however, and do not compress as well as down for packing.

When shopping for bags, check their ratings. Some will keep you warm at 15 degrees, some at zero, and some at even lower. Consider your needs and purchase accordingly. If you'll be camping in warm weather, its needless to pack around the bulk and extra weight of a sub-zero bag. Be sure to pack your bag so that it doesn't get wet. A simple way is to seal it tightly in a couple heavy duty garbage bags.

No matter how warm your sleeping bag, don't forget some

sort of pad to sleep on. Air mattresses and foam pads provide both warmth and cushion for a comfortable night's sleep.

Emergency Kit

This kit should always be included on an extended hunting trip. It should be small enough to carry, and accommodate the following:

- **Space blanket for protection against cold and wet**
- **Waterproof container of matches**
- **Miscellaneous first-aid kit**
- **Steel wool for fire starting**
- **Dehydrated or dried high-energy foods**
- **Backup compass and knife**
- **Signal mirror and whistle**
- **Any prescription medicines or spare eyeglasses.**

Depending on the circumstances, you may add some items such as extra water, a snake-bite kit, or warm clothes.

Field Dressing Gear

If you are hunting big game on foot, take along a pack frame to help carry out your game meat and trophy. The following items will make butchering and field dressing game an easy task.

- **Knife and hone**–A sharp folding or fixed-blade knife is needed to field dress game and skin the carcass. Avoid excessively large knives in favor of a small sturdy one which makes the job easier. A sharpening stone of some sort is necessary. Dull knives make the job needlessly difficult.
- **Rope and cord**–A 20 to 30-food section of nylon rope is handy for dragging, positioning, or hanging bagged game. Cord or twine can be used for a multitude of uses including tying off the rectum while field dressing.
- **Block and tackle**–A small bock and tackle may be necessary for working with larger game such as moose or elk.
- **Meat bags or cheesecloth**–It's a good idea to carry sturdy plastic bags whenever you hunt. These bags are handy for containing small animal carcasses or hearts and livers of big game. In warm weather, a game bag of breathable material such as cheesecloth is ideal for keeping flies away from a big game carcass.
- **Small folding saw or hatchet**–A folding saw or hatchet may come in handy for certain steps in dressing, such as splitting an animal's pelvis.

You may need more or less equipment depending on what and where your hunting. If you're hunting backcountry where you can't get to a taxidermist quickly, don't forget to bring salt to preserve your trophy's cape or hide. In addition, if you'll be caping your own trophy for the taxidermist, bring a tape measure to record the size of your trophy's neck and head to ensure the correct size mount. Also, some hunters wear disposable plastic gloves while field-dressing game. Consider your needs and pack gear accordingly.

Equipment Considerations

Miscellaneous tools and camping gear may be necessary depending on where and what your hunting. A few items you may want to include on your list are:

- **Bow and Spare Parts**
- **Arrows and Bow Shooting Gear**
- **Knife**
- **Compass and Maps**
- **Binoculars**
- **Decoys, Scents, and Calls**
- **Tool Kit**
- **Toilet Paper**
- **Sleeping Bag, Pad, and Pillow**
- **Flashlight**
- **Extra Batteries and Fuel**
- **Tent, Stakes**
- **Camp Stove**
- **First Aid Kit, Snake Bite Kit**
- **Fire-Building Materials**
- **Heater, Fuel**
- **Prescription Medications**
- **Water**
- **Spare Clothing**
- **Food and Drink**
- **Rope**
- **Saw or Axe**
- **Spare Eyeglasses**
- **Cooking and Eating Utensils**
- **Shave Kit, Wash Cloth, Towel**
- **Camera and Film**
- **Cooler**
- **Plastic Bags**

Part II
Bow Shooting for Hunters

CHAPTER 4

SHOOTING THE HUNTING BOW

M an has been shooting bows and arrows for about 25,000 years. Nearly every primitive society on Earth developed the bow and arrow on its own, and its people used archery gear every day through most of its existence.

Maybe it's because of all this "practice" that most people are fascinated by bows and arrows and have a knack for shooting them. For many of us, the ability to pick up a bow and arrow and shoot reasonably close to our target seems locked in our genes.

If you wish to become a successful bowhunter, you must learn, practice and refine this natural ability until you can

Photo by Richard P. Smith

Will you be able to make the shot at the moment of truth? That'll depend on how familiar you are with shooting fundamentals, how much you've practiced, and the quality of that practice.

consistently put arrows into an area the size of the animal's vital zone, at ranges you can consistently approach to the animal. Your bowhunting accuracy will depend partly on equipment, shooting conditions, and other factors, but shooting technique is most important.

Photo by Karl Gunzer Jr.

Bow Shooting Basics

Accurate archery demands a set of consistencies. Even extraordinarily talented instinctive shooters must draw, anchor, sight, release, and follow through the same way each time they shoot. There are other factors in shooting, but performing each of these basic shooting steps consistently and in a way that promotes accuracy is the key to becoming an accomplished archer.

A good bow shot starts with good form. This involves the positioning of the feet, wrist and hands, your grip on the bow, and a consistent anchor point. Let your back and shoulder muscles, rather than your arm, do most of the work.

Shooting Position

A good shot begins with a good shooting position. While your actual position in hunting situations will vary—you may be standing, seated, or kneeling—your upper body form can and should be consistent through each of these positions. This leads to the most consistent draw length, sight picture, anchor point, and string travel. If these vary, the arrow thrust or your sight picture will vary, and that will hurt accuracy.

As you learn to shoot, the basic position is to stand almost sideways to the target, feet about shoulder width, with your body turned just a bit to the target. Find a comfortable posture, one that feels natural. Later, you can practice from other positions. No matter what your stance is, the relative positions of your arms and upper body should stay the same. Be especially careful when shooting from a tree stand that you keep all upper body elements in the same relative position. Aim downward not by lowering your arms, but by bending at the waist.

Grip

Your grip on the bow handle plays an important part in being able to develop accuracy. If you hold the bow in a way that applies sideways pressure, the bow will twist a bit as you release. If this twist varies, each arrow will be sent on a slightly different course. If your grip changes up or down, it will also affect the way the arrow leaves the bow. The secret is to hold the bow in a way that creates no twisting pressure, and to hold it the same way for each shot. This can best be accomplished by cradling the handle riser in the palm of your hand, rather than actually gripping the bow as you would a baseball bat. Use just enough finger pressure to keep from dropping the bow. Some archers use a wrist strap to help them hold the bow with little gripping pressure.

Draw

There are several methods of drawing the bow. Most archers, and nearly all compound bow shooters, use a straight-draw method. A right-handed shooter holds the bow with his left arm nearly straight, keeping his eye on the target and the bow close to the correct shooting position as he draws. There are other slight variations to drawing the bow. Some shooters, especially those using a bow that is difficult for them to draw, elevate the bow and bring it down as they draw. This may be a slightly more comfortable way to draw, but is not practical if your target is a nervous game animal that may bolt because of the exaggerated movement.

Some archers, especially instinctive shooters, draw in a pushpull manner. They start with the bow a few inches from their body, drawing the string and straightening their bow arm at the same time.

For some instinctive shooters, the draw is part of the sighting process. They move the bow to the correct hold as the string comes back, and release as they reach full draw. Most bowhunters reach their anchor point before they begin calculating the best hold.

Anchor Point

The anchor point may be the most vital element of the bow shot. This point—the spot where you hold your string hand each time you shoot—must be precisely consistent. A variation up or down will change the trajectory of your arrow. A variation forward or backward will change the amount of thrust on your arrow. Moving it away from the face will send arrows to the left for a right-hander, to the right for a left-hander.

The anchor point, like many things in archery, should be what works best for you. Find a way of positioning your string hand at your face consistently. This usually means touching

Photo by Mike Strandlund

A consistent anchor point is crucial to consistent shooting. Your drawing hand must come back to the same position each time, touching the tip of your chin, corner of your mouth, or some other reference point.

your index finger or mechanical release to the corner of your mouth, a point on your jaw, or just under your eye.

Your hold at anchor point must remain rock-steady through your sighting and release. The various methods of sighting in archery are discussed later in this chapter under their own subheadings.

Release

Releasing the arrow must be accomplished with utmost smoothness and consistency. There should be no forward or backward movement of the string or your hand until the string rolls off the finger tips or springs from the release mechanism. Then your string hand should spring backward a bit with the sudden release of string pressure.

It is important that you release precisely when you want to, which for many archers is not as easy as it sounds. "Target panic" is the name of a rather common affliction among archers, a psychological block that makes them release before they have a perfect sight picture, or entirely keeps them from aligning properly.

Several factors, including excitement, physical discomfort or fatigue and other factors common in hunting situations can lead to inconsistent releases. This may include plucking the string or letting it creep, moving the hand away from the face or otherwise changing the way the string is released, all of which make it impossible for an accurate shot. Having the training and concentration to make consistently smooth releases under the stress of a hunting situation is important to good hunting accuracy.

Follow-Through

As the string jumps forward and the arrow flies, maintain your form until the arrow hits the target. Keep your eyes open and on the target, freeze your stance, and keep the bow as steady as possible during recoil. This is called follow-through, and is one of the most important factors in shooting the bow accurately.

Photo by Karl Gunzer Jr.

Hold your draw until your sight picture is perfect. Release smoothly, keeping your eyes open and moving your bow arm as little as possible until the arrow hits the target.

Sighting Techniques

There are several very different ways of shooting a bow, which fit into two general categories: shooting with a sighting device, and shooting without one. Any of the methods are fine for the bowhunter, as long as he has developed acceptable accuracy with the method and does not try to exceed his limitations.

Whether you shoot with or without sights, one factor remains constant in all sighting methods. Concentrate full attention on the target or, more correctly, the exact part of the target you wish to hit. "Pick a spot" is common bowhunting advice and will benefit instinctive shooters and sight shooters alike. Any bowhunter who believes it's impossible to miss a point-blank shot at a big game animal is naive. Not only is it possible but it's quite likely unless you focus your full attention on putting your arrow exactly where you want it to go. Here's where a sight pin may best benefit a shooter by forcing concentration. Regardless, a composed "sightless" shooter who picks a spot on the target may deliver an arrow with equal accuracy and effectiveness.

Shooting with Sights

The great majority of today's archers use a sighting aid to shoot their bows. The advantage of using a sight is that it brings mechanical precision into play; you don't just estimate, as with instinctive shooting. The disadvantage is that bow sights will put the arrow in precisely the *wrong* place if you misjudge distance or make another error.

Pin Sights

The most popular type of bow sight is the multiple-pin sight. This device usually has four or five pins, mounted vertically on the handle riser, each corresponding to a certain yardage. The shooter selects the pin that corresponds with the yardage to the target, holds the pin on-target while aligning it with the bow string or a rear peep sight, and keeps it there as he releases.

To set up this type of sight, the shooter mounts the steel sight bracket on his bow, marks off yardages, and tries different pin positions as he shoots practice arrows. The rule for setting sight pins is to move the pin in the opposite direction you want the arrow to go—move the pin up if you want to shoot lower, move it to the left to shoot farther to the right, and vice-versa.

Photo by Mike Strandlund

When shooting with multiple pin sights, anchor the tip of the correct pin on the exact spot you want to hit.

The shooter must memorize the yardage for each of the pins. The upper pins will be for closer range, and the lower pins for longer shots. If the shooter knows the exact yardage, and it falls between the setting of his pins, he may hold one pin higher or lower, or concentrate on shooting with the gap between pins on-target.

Some shooters use only a single pin, set to a certain distance, and adjust its position while aiming to compensate for variances in distance to the target. This was common practice before modern archery innovations. Some longbow and recurve shooters simply taped a nail or similar object to their bow and used it as a sight pin.

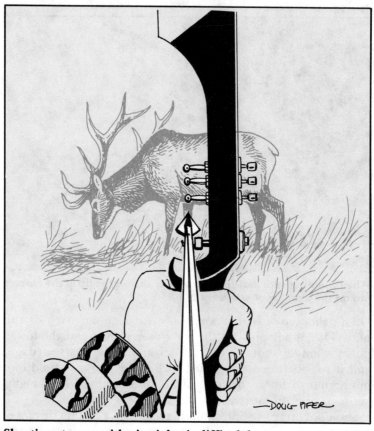

Shooting at game with pin sights is difficult because you must pick the exact spot on the animal you want to hit. Practice by shooting at life-size game targets without bullseyes.

Other Bowsights

A variation of the single-pin sight is the adjustable-pin design now made by several companies and becoming quite popular. This is a device with a single sight pin with a mechanism that allows instant vertical movement of the pin. It is attached to an indicator and a yardage index; the hunter sets the pointer on the correct yardage, and the pin automatically moves to the correct position.

The pendulum tree stand sight also uses a single sight, but with a completely different concept. The sight pivots on a swivel as the bow is raised or lowered to different angles, and is designed to adjust automatically as yardages vary. With the unlimited variety of bows, stand heights, and other factors, there can be some obvious problems with this sight doing what it's supposed to. But when it does, it is very accurate.

Another type of sight is the bow scope, which may or may not give slight magnification and a single sight set for a fixed distance. These are usually not as useful for hunting as multiple-yardage sights, because they don't accurately address all shooting ranges. There are also sights with several crosshairs, which work on the same principle as the pin sight.

Shooting Without Sights

Although many modern-day bowhunters favor a bow sight, shooting bows and arrows without benefit of any sighting mechanism was standard practice for many centuries. It's still a deadly effective means of shooting a hunting bow. Some veteran bowhunters shoot instinctively, or with an apparent spontaneity that puzzles onlookers unfamiliar with instinctive shooting methods.

Actually, good bare-bow shooters may have several advantages over shooters who use a bow sight. Sights were first developed and used by target archers who stood at fixed distances from a target and shot arrow after arrow into a stationary target. Bowhunters seldom know the exact distance to their target. The target is capable of moving, and often allows little time for readjusting aim. In hunting, the target shooter's ability to tightly group arrows in a tiny bullseye is not as important as putting the first arrow in the right spot. Further, having to estimate yardage, then select the proper sight pin, draw, anchor, aim, and release, may take more time than an animal will allow.

There are some disadvantages to shooting without sights. Bare-bow shooters usually need more time to develop their shooting skill and regular practice to keep that skill honed. Some shooters simply don't have the knack to shoot by judgment alone. It is much easier to make mental errors and go into a shooting "slump" when you rely so heavily on judgment.

Instinctive Shooting

Instinctive shooting is shooting by pure judgment--you use no sights and no points of reference. Like throwing a baseball, it is done by feel and is a combination of innate and learned skills. Practice develops a sense or feeling for how the arrow will fly, imprinting in the shooter's mind a picture of the arrow's trajectory as it speeds to its target.

Shooting instinctively requires the shooter to concentrate on the spot he wants to hit and shooting "feel," using muscle memory rather than points of reference for aiming.

To become a good instinctive shooter, you should practice under realistic hunting conditions after you've mastered the mechanics of shooting a bow. Through proper practice—such as stump shooting—you'll learn to intuitively judge distances, which is exactly what happens when you develop the "feel" of instinctive shooting. You stare hard at a small spot on the target, and can picture the arrow's flight in any situation you may encounter. Each time you draw an arrow for a shot, you let your mind do the rest.

Instinctive shooting is often harder to learn and more effort is generally required to keep shooting abilities sharp. Yet any bowhunter possesses the ability to shoot instinctively. It is ideally suited to bowhunting, especially where quick shots at unknown yardages are required. Knowledge and practice are the keys.

Pure instinctive shooting has been called "aiming and shooting by feel." Instinctive shooters explain they do not consciously judge the distance to the target or aim by using any reference point. They simply raise their bow, draw their arrow and, when everything "feels" right, they release.

Knowledge of your equipment allows you to picture arrow trajectory before the shot is made. Repeated practice sessions make you understand that when an animal is 18 yards away you don't elevate your bow as much as when shooting at a target 36 yards away. Yet in pure instinctive shooting you unconsciously lower or raise your bow and automatically because you *know* how and when to shoot. Again, it *feels* right so you release. That's instinctive shooting.

As noted, everyone has some instinctive shooting ability, which may be developed through repeated practice. If you doubt that, think of learning to throw a baseball or football—or shoot a basketball.

When you've practiced to the point that shooting by "feel" is natural, you'll shoot arrows automatically and accurately without mental effort. Concentrate on the target—whether standing, running or even flying—and release when you sense the time is right. People who shoot with the aid of sights find such shots difficult if not impossible.

What works well for one shooter won't work well for another. Some people lack the natural skills—or the hand/eye coordination—of others. A few may even have themselves convinced there's no way they can shoot without the aid of some sort of sighting device. Others simply do not have the time to acquire and perfect instinctive shooting skills. Such individuals are likely to find instinctive shooting downright difficult. And although it's not impossible for them, the fact is they may be better off shooting with a sight or using another variation of the instinctive shooting method.

Gap Shooting

While shooting by "feel" may seem to be an oversimplified definition of instinctive shooting, the fact is it's accurate. Yet there are some shooters who shun the use of mechanical sights on their bows but rely on sighting devices of another sort to aim. Gap shooting is one such peripheral aiming method.

A gap shooter typically uses the point of his arrow as the sight. He has practiced enough that he knows where to hold the arrow tip above or below the target. For example, when he shoots at 10 yards the point of his arrow may be below an animal's chest by a foot or more. When the target is 20 yards away the arrow point may be on the exact spot the shooter wants to hit. And when the animal is 30 yards away, the arrow point may be at or above the top of the back in line with the point of impact.

This method combines instinctive and sight shooting techniques. Many gap shooters do not estimate yardages but like pure instinctive shooters release when the point of their arrow looks to be in position and the shot "feels" right. Regardless, they do use their arrow tip as a sight of sorts and aim with it before shifting attention to the target itself and releasing.

Gun Barreling

A final noteworthy method used by some archers involves a technique called "gun barreling." Sometimes tabbed "Apache-style" shooting, it involves sighting down the arrow the way you would sight down a shotgun barrel before pulling the trigger. In gun barreling, it is necessary for the shooter to change his anchor point to a position just below the eye. This method works well with practice; however, most shots are limited to shorter distances. As with gap and point-of-aim shooting, the technique relies on an aiming device of sorts and cannot be considered truly instinctive shooting.

If you use a sightless aiming system, get to know your equipment thoroughly. Learn your effective shooting range and limit your shots to that. Use the same bow, arrows and broadheads you'll use in hunting. Resist the temptation to change equipment at the last moment. Any such changes are likely to affect the information you've collected in your mental files and will force you to relearn the data before your instinctive shooting ability returns to its former level.

Instinctive shooting is not for every bowhunter. But for those who recognize its advantages and are willing to learn, it represents both a challenge and an opportunity.

Refining Your Accuracy

Quality Practice

There is a world of difference between placing an arrow into a paper target and into a live animal. Though shooting at stationary, inanimate targets from known distances may help you master proper archery technique and form, you should realize there are better ways to prepare for hunting big game.

Photo by Karl Gunzer Jr.

Archery practice should emphasize quality over quantity. Rather than long practice sessions spaced apart, shoot a few arrows every few days, pretending that each arrow you loose is at that trophy animal of a lifetime.

A good technique for practice is to shoot only a *few* arrows. Most bowhunters shoot far too many arrows. In actuality, you seldom have many opportunities in the field. The goal of any serious bowhunter should be to shoot a few arrows consistently on target. Be able to make your first arrow count from any distance. In practice, it's much better to shoot six arrows every day than 60 arrows once a week.

Most bowhunters have a place where they can put up a target

or some straw bales and practice as much as they want. Even if you don't have such a place, many opportunities exist for bowhunters to practice shooting. Many bowhunting and field archery clubs offer ranges, including broadhead targets, designed to improve shooting skills. Also, many indoor archery ranges throughout the U.S. offer year-round bowhunting practice and hunting-league shooting.

If you decide to practice on your own, take every precaution to insure your own as well as others' safety. Urban areas aren't conducive for archery practice, but if you do decide to give it a try, make sure you have a large, open area with good visibility. Also be sure to use a solid backstop for arrows. Some public parks have archery targets available. Be aware that many urban areas have ordinances against shooting bows outside of established ranges.

Practice in a way that closely resembles a hunting situation. Wear hunting clothing, and shoot from hunting ranges and positions. Imagine you are actually shooting at an animal. If you visualize properly, you can actually feel the excitement of the hunt as you draw and release. You can get used to that feeling and learn to shoot accurately in that frame of mind. And when that trophy buck *is* finally standing there in bow range, you'll feel like you've been through it a thousand times, and be less likely to "choke."

It's also a good idea to practice shooting from the positions you'll likely find yourself in when hunting. (In most cases, standing fully erect and coming to full draw is not the usual hunting position you'll take in the field.) Practicing from many different—even awkward—positions prepares you to take any shot you're given. If you plan to hunt from a tree stand, practice shooting from elevated positions. Remember to practice at different times of day and under different weather conditions.

Perhaps the best way to practice for bowhunting is to go stump shooting. Alone or with a hunting partner, walk through woodlands and fields, selecting rotting stumps, clumps of grass, a fallen leaf, a shadow—anything that offers a good, safe shot—and try to place your first arrow in that predetermined target.

Proper practice for instinctive shooters involves releasing a single arrow from various distances and positions. While all shooters realize that the proper shooting technique includes the stance, grip, draw, anchor, aim, release and follow-through, they understand that many variations exist. These basic steps are just that--basic. Once the preliminary steps are mastered to the point they become routine, a shooter may begin to personalize his style and develop his ability to its fullest.

Roving through a wooded area, a shooter may take a kneeling shot at a rotten stump 21 yards away. As he retrieves his arrow, he stands and shoots at a tuft of grass poking through the leaves 13 yards to his left, then twists his body and releases another arrow at a dead leaf 33 yards across a shallow ravine. As he walks, he shoots uphill and down, at all yardages within his effective shooting range. He practices the kinds of shots he may encounter during an actual hunt—and he hones his ability to quickly and accurately place his arrows in targets of his choosing.

Always practice with your hunting equipment and, if possible, dress in the same clothes and footwear you will wear when actually hunting. Shoot uphill, downhill, between trees and over brush, learning to concentrate when releasing your arrow.

As hunting season approaches, test-shoot your broadheads (hunting heads generally fly differently than field points) and practice with them exclusively. This way you'll be able to check flight characteristics and the overall performance of your broadheads in relation to your bow. Shoot at life-size animal targets, picking a spot and placing your arrow in the kill area from different shooting positions and varying distances. Keep practice sessions short, enjoyable. Frequent periods of brief practice are usually more beneficial than extended, infrequent sessions.

A pile of fine sand or styrofoam blocks make excellent broadhead targets. Just make sure to change replaceable blades and resharpen fixed blades before you actually use them in the field. Remember, sharp broadheads are the foremost factor for successful bowhunting.

Such practice under realistic bowhunting conditions helps concentration and hones the ability to judge distances accurately. With the right practice, you'll be able to make that one shot you'll get.

Photo by Richard P. Smith

Take a few practice shots on each bowhunting outing you make. This practice—matching hunting conditions exactly—is the best practice.

CHAPTER 5

BOW PERFORMANCE AND TUNING

S ome beginning bowhunters assume they can buy a mail-order bow, a cheap set of shafts and broadheads, and immediately begin shooting and hunting. Wrong.

Photo by Mike Strandlund

A fine-tuned shooting set-up will maximize your accuracy, prevent malfunctions, and give best arrow penetration.

Under normal conditions the best bow, arrows, broadhead and accessories will be of little use unless they are all well-matched and adjusted for accurate, consistent performance. This step is called tuning, and is crucial for the accuracy and arrow performance necessary for quick kills with a bow. It becomes more and more important as the scope and complexity of archery gear increases yearly.

Bow Tuning

The first step in setting up your bow and arrow is adjusting your bow to perform well and match your personal requirements. In all the steps involved in tuning and maintaining a bow, be sure to consult manufacturer's recommendations. The owner's manual will point out correct procedures.

Draw Weight

Draw length and weight are the most important bow considerations. Give careful consideration to the draw weight you want your bow to be. A bow that is too light will provide less arrow speed and energy, adversely affecting accuracy and penetration, and possibly cause releases to be sloppy. A bow too heavy may be difficult to shoot accurately, and unpleasant to shoot. You may find a bow tough to pull on the target range is impossible to get back under adverse shooting conditions—when you're cold, tired, or nervous—and it may cost you an animal. Most hunting bows for adults are between 55 and 70 pounds. Keep in mind that with practice comes increased strength—you'll be able to handle a heavier bow the more you shoot, but be realistic regarding your physical limitations.

Draw Length

At the same time you determine the draw weight, you need to figure your draw length, as described in Chapter 1. You'll buy your bow—whether compound or stick bow—according to its weight at a certain length. Most compounds are adjustable for a certain amount of weight and length; recurves and longbows are usually sold at a certain weight at a draw length of 28 inches. If your draw is longer or shorter, you must figure two or three pounds difference in pull for every inch your draw length varies from 28 inches.

To adjust the length and weight of a compound's draw, refer to the bow's owner's manual. The draw length of most compounds can be adjusted by changing the position of the string ends or cables on the wheels. Poundage is usually changed by turning the bolt that attaches the limb to the riser with an Allen wrench. In most cases, a couple turns to the right will

Photo by Karl Gunzer Jr.

Obtain and read an owner's manual for your bow before making any adjustments. Each model of bow is different, and you can damage your's by using an improper procedure.

increase the draw weight by a couple of pounds; turns to the left decreases the weight. After a half-turn or so, the bolt on the other limb should be turned, to keep pressures on the bow even. Again, bows are getting more complicated each year, requiring new or different procedures, so consult your owner's manual.

Brace Height

Setting correct brace height is another important step in adjusting a bow. Brace height is the distance between the pressure point on the handle and the string when the bow is strung but not drawn. A low brace height (string closer to the handle) will give you a little more arrow velocity, because the power stroke is a bit longer. But because the arrow stays attached to the string for a few milliseconds longer and is not released until it makes a tighter angle to the handle, movement of the bow at the time of release is more critical and accuracy may suffer. The opposite holds true for a high brace height (string farther from the handle). Long-limbed bows usually have lower brace height that short-limbed ones, but each bow performs best with a certain compromise in brace height. Follow manufacturer's recommendations, and experiment with slight changes in brace height until you find what works best for you.

Tiller

Another adjustment you must make on your bow is setting the tiller. Tiller is the distance from a limb to the string. On stick bows, there should be a slight difference in distance from the middle of the top limb straight across to the string, compared to the distance from the bottom limb to the string. This difference is necessary because of uneven pressure put on the limbs during the draw, especially for a finger-shooter. In most cases, proper tiller results in the bottom limb being a bit closer to

Photo by Karl Gunzer Jr.

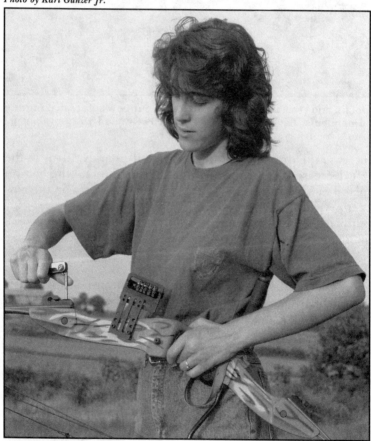

On most compound bows, the draw weight and tiller can easily be adjusted with an Allen wrench.

the string than the top limb. In essence, the bottom limb exerts more pull than the top.

Most compound bow manufacturers, however, recommend that tiller should be about equal for each limb of a compound. To check the tiller on your bow, measure from the top and the bottom of the riser straight across to the string. The top limb should be equal to or perhaps an eighth-inch farther from the string than the bottom limb. You may experiment with slight changes in tiller that may give you better results.

Limb and Wheel Performance

One factor which determines how well you can shoot a particular compound bow is the performance of the limbs and wheels. For an archer to feel comfortable with and get full accuracy potential from a bow, he must be satisfied that the draw and power stroke of the bow is "smooth," a general term for many factors in the draw and cast.

In recurves and longbows, smoothness begins with how evenly the bow increases in weight as it is drawn. Ideally, a stick bow should increase in weight evenly as it is drawn. A bow that increases drastically in poundage as the string approaches the anchor point is said to "stack." This makes the draw uncomfortable and the release more sensitive. Any slight variation in the archer's draw length on a particular shot will add or subtract a significant amount of poundage with a bow that stacks badly, with great harm to accuracy. There is very little that can be done to remedy a badly stacking bow, outside of shortening your draw length, which will have other adverse effects. The best prevention for this problem is to give a bow a good try-out before buying it, to be sure it has a smooth draw.

When the string returns to its brace position upon release, there is a certain amount of shock and vibration. Some bows have a lot, some have very little. This can be adjusted—by changing brace height, arrow weight, bow weight (by adding a stabilizer or other accessories to the bow) and other factors.

Compounds operate on a different principle. Most use round or cam-shaped wheels, with an off-center axle, as a combination pulley-lever arrangement. As the shooter draws, the wheels rotate inward and bow weight increase rapidly for the first eight inches or so until "peak weight" is reached. Then there is a quick decline in draw weight until the "valley," or peak let-off, is reached. Thereafter, draw weight again increases, this time very rapidly, at the stage commonly described as the "wall."

There are several important points here. The shooter's anchor point must coincide with the bottom of the valley, or he will be holding more weight than he should be. The wheels must rotate evenly, or bad performance will result. If you believe that you may have problems in this area, check your draw length, and have a friend check that the wheels are coinciding by putting marks on the wheels and watching that they rotate together during the draw. If the wheels are not synchronized, a trip to the repair shop is in order.

Silencing

A final important step in tuning a hunting bow is achieving quiet performance. A well tuned bow will usually shoot fairly quietly, but the only way to be sure is through test shooting.

Stick bows are generally the quietest shooting because of their minimum number of parts. Compounds, on the other hand, have many parts and attachments to rattle and vibrate. Shooters who insist on shooting ultralight arrows add to this problem. Common causes of bow noise include the bowstring, quivers, sights, cables, limb bolts, and arrow rests.

The most common bow noise from both stick bows and compounds is string twang. This is easily remedied by attaching silencers such as puffs of yarn or rubber whiskers to the string.

Vibrating parts such as quivers and bowsights can usually be quieted with a good tightening of all bolts. Be sure arrows are securely mounted in the quiver and don't contact the bow upon release. Short quivers generally vibrate more than long ones. Tighten all sight pins and check them periodically to ensure they don't vibrate loose with shooting.

Cables vibrating upon release is another common noise problem among compounds. The easiest remedy is to add a cable slide to dampen vibrations. If this doesn't work, you may have problems with cables contacting the limbs, wheels, or yolk mounts, and a trip to a knowledgeable archery dealer is probably the best remedy.

If you use an arrow rest, be sure to mount it tightly to the bow, so it doesn't rattle or vibrate upon release. Usually the simplest rests make the least noise. Cover any metal parts that touch the arrow with shrink tubing or moleskin to ensure minimal noise as you draw your bow. The scraping of an aluminum arrow on a rest has been the demise of many shooting opportunities.

Finally, test shoot your bow, paying attention to any noise while drawing and shooting. Be sure the bow doesn't squeak or pop while drawing. If it does, check the limb mounts and wheels for proper lubrication. If the bow makes a great deal of noise upon release, and you're shooting a light arrow, you may have to select a heavier shaft to quiet your bow.

Matching Arrows

As described in Chapter 2, arrows must be flexible. For their light mass, they undergo a tremendous amount of shock when the string is released. To fly straight, they must have the right amount of flex to bend around the arrow rest or bow handle so that they may recover and fly true after they leave the bow.

Arrow stiffness is described as spine. This is affected mainly by the diameter (and with hollow aluminum shafts, the wall thickness) of the arrow, but there are several factors other than the actual flexibility of the shaft that determine spine. Longer arrows and those with heavier tips will bend more on string release than the exact same shaft that is shorter or tipped with a lighter head. The tension of a cushion plunger will also determine the effective spine.

Arrow manufacturers have charts that indicate the proper type of shaft to use, depending on the type and weight of your bow, your draw length and tip weight. This is a good place to start, and will likely provide you with the best match-up of arrow and bow. But you'll have to do some experimenting to determine if your setup gives you optimum arrow flight.

Achieving Good Arrow Flight

Locating the Nock Point

The nock point—the spot on the string where the arrow is placed—is important in getting good arrow flight. If the nock point is too high, the arrow will leave the bow nock-high. If the nock is too low, it will leave either nock-low or, when the rear of the arrow bounces off the arrow rest, nock high.

To determine nock point, you'll need a bow square. This tool clamps to the string with its extension resting on the arrow rest, and shows the user the location of the point on the string that is square with the arrow rest, and measurements up and down the string.

Placement of the nock point depends on many variables, including the bow, the shooter's release style, type of fletching and arrow rest. Most bow makers recommend setting the nock locator—a metal and rubber band clamped to the string—one-quarter to one-half inch above square. When the arrow is placed under this nock locator, the bottom of the shaft will be a little higher than square with the arrow rest. This is necessary to keep fletching from striking the arrow rest.

Paper testing—described later in this chapter—will determine if the nock point should be lowered or raised above this starting point for optimum arrow flight.

Photo by Mike Strandlund

Use a bow square to locate a starting point for your nock set—usually about ³⁄₈-inch above 90 degrees to the arrow rest. Test shooting will show if it needs adjustment from there.

Centershot Adjustment

Most archers benefit from using an adjustable arrow rest to position the arrow shaft closer or farther from the bow handle. Theoretically, the rest should be adjusted so the arrow points directly away from the string upon release. This is usually true when the shooter uses a mechanical release, which can loose the string flawlessly. But most bowhunters release the string with their fingers, which puts torque on the string and increases the bending of the arrow. In this case, it is usually better if the arrow angles slightly away from the bow in relation to the string (to the left for a right-handed shooter).

To adjust for this alignment on stick bows, first hang your bow with a string or prop it up against an object so it stands vertically. Place the arrow in position on the arrow rest and string. Stand behind the string and examine the alignment. With the string lined up with the center of the limbs and the

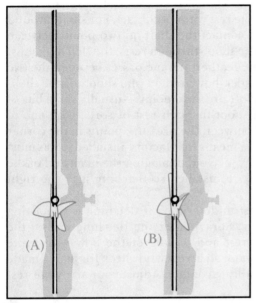

To get the best arrow flight possible, (A) the arrow should point straight away from the string for a release shooter, (B) a little to the left for a right-handed finger shooter.

(A)   (B)

handle, the arrow shaft should point a little to the left (just enough so that you can see the full width of the arrow point) if you're a right-handed archer. If alignment isn't correct, adjust your arrow rest or plunger until it is.

To make initial centershot adjustments with a compound, first measure the distance from the string to the left side of the limbs at the limb tips. Midway on each limb, measure that same distance from the left side of the limb toward the center of the limb. Make a heavy, vertical mark there. Now prop the bow up with the arrow on the string, stand back and align the string with the vertical marks, and check where the arrow points. It should point straight away from the string for a release shooter, a little to the left for a right-handed finger shooter. (Note: This method applies only if your bow limbs are the same width at the tips and the center.)

Paper-testing will help you fine-tune this adjustment.

Testing Fletch Clearance

If arrow fletching strikes any part of the arrow rest or bow handle as the shaft leaves the bow, it will be thrown slightly off course. This results in less than ideal arrow flight and prevents optimum accuracy. Nearly all arrow rests will allow arrow fletching to pass the rest and riser with no contact, if proper adjustments are made.

Arrow nocks must be installed so that fletching sits at the proper angle to pass the rest without contact. For shoot-around rests, the rest should contact the shaft on two points between two of the fletches. For shoot-through rests, the fletching must be aligned so that one feather or vane passes between the two pressure points. For stick-bow archers who shoot off the shelf, there should be two soft pressure points—usually small bits of carpet—that form a shoot-through rest of sorts, with one of the feathers passing between the pressure points in the corner of the shelf. This often means that factory-installed nocks must be removed (carefully, to avoid damaging the nock end of the arrow) and new nocks reinstalled so fletching is at the right angle.

Use the powder test to determine if fletching is contacting any part of your bow. Spray either the fletching end of the arrow or the arrow rest and handle of the bow with white foot-powder spray. Shoot an arrow, and check for marks made in the powder that indicate contact. Adjust your arrows or rest accordingly.

Testing Arrow Flight

When the bow and arrows are not matched or adjusted correctly, poor arrow flight results. The arrow may wobble up and down (called porpoising) or it may wobble left to right (known as fishtailing). While the quality of your arrow flight will be apparent in target shooting, there are better ways to test the compatibility of your bow and arrows. The easiest and most reliable way is through paper-tuning, which tells you if your arrows are flying straight and assists you in correcting

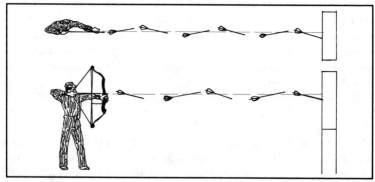

Left to right arrow wobble is known as fishtailing, while up and down wobble is called porpoising. Both must be minimized to ensure good accuracy.

flight problems. It helps you make fine adjustments in nock location, centershot adjustment, and arrow spine.

With paper tuning, fletched arrows with field points of the same weight as the broadheads you plan to use are shot through paper into a backstop more than a full arrow length behind the paper. Do initial testing about three or four yards from the paper; then move back to 10 or 15 yards and try it again.

Tears in the paper indicate where the fletching passed through the paper in relation to the point. If you're shooting right-handed and the tears show the nock went left of the tip, the arrow is spined too light. You must lower your draw weight or increase cushion tension on your arrow rest, use shorter arrows, lighter tips, or try a stiffer shaft. If the nock tears to the right, the spine is probably too great, and you need to increase draw weight or decrease cushion tension, use longer arrows, heavier tips or a lighter shaft. Arrows with a low nock impact indicate the nock point is set too low; those with a high nock indicate the nock point is either too low or too high.

If you shoot off the shelf of a stick bow or use a non-adjustable arrow rest, you are limited in the ways you can achieve proper arrow spine for your bow. Here's one way: Start with arrows of the proper spine but longer than you would normally shoot. Test shoot the arrows, which at the longer length should

Photo by Karl Gunzer Jr.

Paper tuning shows if your arrow is flying straight. You can tell by the way an arrow tears through the target if your arrows are spined correctly and if your bow needs adjustment.

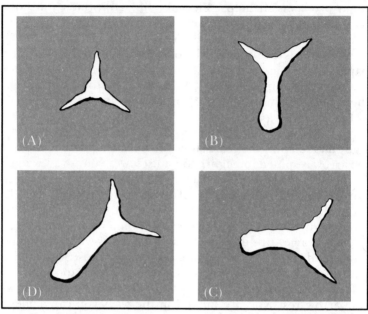

A perfect hole with three fletching tears (A) indicates perfect arrow flight. A vertical tear (B) indicates improper nock height, while horizontal tears (C) indicate improper centershot. Tears both vertical and horizontal (D) should be corrected by adjusting nock height first, then arrow rest tension or alignment. Keep in mind improperly sized arrows may keep you from attaining good arrow flight, no matter how you adjust your bow.

be a little light in spine. Alternately shoot them and trim them back a quarter-inch until they reach the correct spine and fly correctly for you.

Arrow Grouping

Once you've achieved good arrow flight and a fair degree of marksmanship with your bow, you can fine-tune your bow and arrows. This involves testing your arrows to see if they all impact at the point of aim.

Start with field points, which are more uniform than broadheads and will give a clearer idea of the performance of your shafts. Shoot all your arrows carefully, at the same yardage—15 or 20 yards is a good range for this test. Well-executed shots should group all shafts very close together. Any arrow that impacts outside of the group should be marked and retested. Arrows that consistently impact outside of the group are probably a little crooked, out of balance, or have a fletching problem. You may try refletching and rotating the nock a bit to see if you can get the shafts to group better. If accuracy remains poor, discard the shaft.

The final tuning step is to test and adjust for broadhead flight. If you have an arrow-straightener or spin-tester available, use it to check for alignment before you begin shooting. Mount the broadhead and give the shaft a spin. Any apparent wobble in the head denotes misalignment, and will likely result in poor accuracy. The problem may be due to a crooked ferrule or an incorrectly installed point adapter.

Perform the paper-tuning test and the grouping test with broadheads, and make any adjustments necessary. Now is when you make your final sight settings. Some advice: shoot each broadhead-tipped arrow at a different bullseye to avoid cutting fletches and damaging arrows.

Photo by Mike Strandlund

At this final stage you are testing the actual hunting accuracy of your setup. Try to simulate actual hunting conditions—shoot with your bow quiver and arrows installed, wear hunting clothes, including hat and gloves, and otherwise match hunting conditions closely. If you plan to hunt primarily from a tree stand, you should experiment, adjust your sights, and practice accordingly.

The final step in tuning your bow and arrows is to shoot under realistic hunting conditions—with broadheads.

Part III
How to Hunt with a Bow

CHAPTER 6
BOWHUNTING BASICS

B owhunting is a special sport requiring special knowledge and equipment. It is—above all else—personally
challenging. If approached with the proper attitude
and understanding, it can be immensely rewarding.

Bowhunting success should not be measured solely in the
number of animals hanging from a game pole. Although a
punched tag and food for the freezer are basic and honorable
hunting goals, most serious bowhunters revel in the challenge
of the hunt itself. If a kill is made, it is often anticlimactic.
What counts is the personal satisfaction gained from pitting
oneself against wild game while armed with one of man's oldest
hunting tools.

This year, only about one bowhunter in 10 will bag his deer.
Yet bowhunting popularity continues to grow. The reasons
are found in the sport's unique challenges and rewards.

Beginning bowhunters should realize there is no real
shortcut to success. To fully understand bowhunting, you must
experience it. No amount of archery practice can adequately
prepare you for the pulse-pounding moment the animal you

Photo by Mike Strandlund

**Successful bowhunting requires patience, dedication, experience,
and a high level of hunting skill—in that order.**

seek steps into shooting range. Nevertheless, proper practice and preparation are essential. Without them no bowhunter should attempt to hunt. Venture afield only when you understand your personal abilities, what your equipment will and will not do, and how game is to be hunted.

Learning to Bowhunt

Consider yourself fortunate if you have an experienced friend who can help you learn to bowhunt. Having someone to hunt with, to answer your questions and to teach you proper techniques, is an ideal situation. But even without the benefit of an individual teacher, you can master the fundamentals if you are serious and willing to shoulder the responsibility.

One excellent program for beginning bowhunters is the standardized 10-hour International Bowhunter Education Program developed by the National Bowhunter Education Foundation. Now offered across the United States, Canada and in several other countries, the course teaches bowhunting fundamentals and responsibilities. It is designed to help participants become better, safer bowhunters in a minimum amount of time.

Another excellent starting point is this manual and the NRA-sponsored clinics held throughout the United States. These clinics are dedicated to educating America's hunters. Here, experienced professionals and trained volunteers conduct educational seminars, answer questions, and help beginners and advanced bowhunters become safer and more skilled.

Many areas have active, well-organized bowhunting clubs that offer instructional bowhunting seminars or seasonal shooting competitions. Most clubs feature outdoor ranges and some host regular "bowhunter shoots" that simulate real hunting conditions. They feature 3-D animal targets, cardboard silhouettes, or paper

Photo by Richard P. Smith

Spend time learning about the natural history of the species you hunt and the habits of individual animals.

animal targets such as the NRA Life-Size Game Targets set up in hunting terrain with shots taken at unknown distances. These shoots are among the best forms of off-season practice. In addition, such clubs are ideal spots for meeting veteran bowhunters who can provide firsthand advice on equipment, shooting, and hunting techniques.

Knowledge of the hunting area is often a prerequisite to consistent success. Year-round scouting trips will acquaint hunters with their territory and help locate new hunting areas while pinpointing game movements and concentrations. Where necessary, permission to hunt is obtained from landowners. Stand sites will be located and necessary licenses and permits will be obtained well in advance of opening day. Consequently, when bowhunters finally go afield, they are committed, confident, and well-prepared. They are ready to bowhunt.

Hunt Preparation

Several ingredients will help you enjoy better bowhunting. Among them are being fully prepared before you take to the woods, so you are the best bowhunter you can be. Other ingredients are a passion to be involved with the sport, a serious approach to selecting a guide, an effective training or conditioning program, the development of your shooting skills, proper equipment selection, and the time and money to pursue the sport. All of these ingredients will be fitted to your individual lifestyle.

A Place to Hunt

More than two-thirds of all hunting in the United States today occurs on private lands, with the hunter required to seek permission from the landowner. According to a 1981 survey by the Future Farmers of America, the major reason farmers post their land is because of "unpleasant" prior experiences with hunters. Common problems cited were litter, theft, and game law violations.

The key to obtaining permission to hunt on private land is to get to know the landowner—and for him to get to know you. However, you want to do this long before the bow season opens. Approach him early in the year, at a time when his schedule is not so busy. Offer to help mend fences, cut firewood, or volunteer to put up "Hunting By Permission" signs. These activities, when done in a sincere manner, will often guarantee a place to hunt.

Physical Training

Training is important if you're planning to travel to unfamiliar terrain. It's also especially important for those preparing for the rigors of big game hunting in the mountains where excellent shooting opportunities can be few and far between. If you're not in condition when they do come your way, you're apt to let them go by the wayside while you're huffing and puffing and suffering from leg cramps.

The best training is any type of effective exercise program that can be done year-round. That way you will always be prepared for the hunting season. When training for big game hunting, your prime concern should be the legs and lungs. Aerobic exercises like running up stairs or jumping rope are your best bet. A selection of other exercises might include deep knee bends, sit-ups, push-ups and isometrics. Even if you don't have time to do all of them, doing only a few will benefit your overall conditioning program.

Many hunters feel they have to take up jogging or a similar aerobic exercise to get in shape. Actually, brisk walking with a weighted pack is sufficient in most cases, and it isn't as strenuous for those who aren't used to vigorous exercise. Swimming is another excellent conditioning activity for the bowhunter.

Don't forget to keep your shooting muscles and eye in shape by shooting your bow on a regular basis.

Hunting Away From Home

If you decide to travel to bowhunt, you'll have to become something of a travel expert. First, you'll have to decide where to hunt. Then, the method of transportation: Will you drive, or fly? Probably it will depend on cost.

Once you've made your plans to get there, think about your arrival. It's important to have either a guide or a local contact to "bring you into camp," so to speak. Allow yourself plenty of time to get settled once you do arrive. A day—or at least half a day—is best before actually beginning the hunt.

Before embarking on a long, extended trip, consider all the possibilities. Of course, double-check season dates and regulations pertaining to equipment, hunter education requirements, and such.

There is little point in investing time and money in a trip when you disregard essentials such as proper clothing and footwear. It's wise to talk to another bowhunter who has hunted the same general area about these things; he can help you decide what gear you'll need to pack (the tendency is to take

Photo by Gabby Barrus

Hunts that involve travel and extended time away from home—especially those that involve wilderness camping—require special planning.

too much). If you don't know of another hunter or a guide, the next best source of information is wildlife agencies and local bowhunters.

Photo by Stan Warren

It can be hard to find a good outfitter who is well-equipped, conscientious about his clients and skilled at getting them game. Make your choice carefully.

To hunt with a guide—or not to hunt with a guide? Usually on hunts to an unfamiliar area, guides are very important. Without a thorough understanding of where you're hunting and what you're hunting, you can get yourself into some dangerous situations that could lead to personal injury or even death.

How do you select a guide? Plan to do thorough research.

A good place to start is with some of the hunting magazines. Many outdoor publications advertise guide services. Once you've found a potential guide for the area and type of hunt you want, write the guide asking about details. This will help you conceptualize the hunt. A follow-up telephone call will supply even more information about the guide and the hunt he offers. Also, obtaining references and contacting hunters who have hunted with that particular guide in the past season is also advised. Note: you should always contact a cross section of both *successful* and *unsuccessful* hunters for a fair appraisal of the guide's services. The conditions of your agreement should be in writing.

In the main, professional guides are straight-forward, honest businessmen. They want you to have a good hunt. Fortunately, the unreliable, dishonest "professionals" comprise a very small number of today's guides.

Understanding Game Animals

Bowhunting success hinges on the hunter's ability to understand the habits, habitat, and behavior of the game he pursues. Learn all you can about your quarry before taking to the forest with bow in hand.

Deer hunting is the cornerstone of modern bowhunting. No matter where you live, you're probably within an hour's drive of a good area to hunt deer. Far more bowhunter-hours are spent pursuing whitetail deer than all other species combined.

At some point in their careers, most hunters decide they want to hunt another species of big game. Black bear, mule deer, elk, antelope, mountain lion, caribou, moose, and mountain goat are exciting challenges for the bowman. The ultra-difficult animals—such as sheep and big bears—should come only after the building blocks are in place. As a hunter, you may gain confidence from the fact that every species of big game has been taken by bow.

Big game animals depend on their nose, ears, and eyes—usually in that order of importance—to detect potential or imminent danger. Keep the following points in mind as you plan your hunt:

Photos by Mike Strandlund

Understanding the superior senses of game animals is crucial to bowhunting success. You must be well versed in using camouflage, scents, and stealth.

- Human odor, when encountered by an animal at close range, is very alarming. Immediate alertness, overt nervousness, and outright panic are typical reactions.
- Unnatural woodland sounds such as the human voice or metallic noises are sure to draw the immediate attention of keen-eared game. Even the raspy sound of an arrow being drawn into shooting position, the slight creaking of a tree stand, or a stick cracking underfoot can tip your hand at the most inopportune moment. All such sounds can spook game.
- Movement is readily detected. A hand brushing away a bothersome insect, a head turning quickly, a bow being drawn—all may attract an animal's attention. Even if the animal does not immediately run, more often than not it will be alerted to a hunter's presence. This makes getting off a good shot extremely difficult. Because a bowhunter should be close to his target to obtain the most effective results, he must continually guard against detection. Common sense combined with a few pre-hunt precautions can benefit you greatly.

Hunting Methods

NRA Staff Photo

Bowhunters have several basic methods of pursuing game, any of which may be the best in a given hunting situation. The three best options include hunting from tree stands, hunting from ground blinds, and still-hunting/stalking.

Tree Stand Hunting

Bowhunters have probably always hunted from trees, but only in the last couple of decades has it become common. The increasing employment of tree stands and skill in their use

A tree stand gives bowhunters several advantages, making them harder for a deer to see or scent, and giving hunters a better angle to spot game and get a shot.

have been major contributors in the increasing success rates of bowhunters.

Trail-watching from elevated positions on tree limbs or stands is by far the most popular and productive method of bowhunting whitetails. Tree stands are also preferred by the vast majority of bear bowhunters, not only to stay undetected, but for safety reasons. Mule deer and other big game species are successfully hunted from elevated stands as well. The basic advantages of this method include the following:

- A bowhunter in a tree generally has a greater field of vision; approaching game is often easier to detect.
- Telltale human scent is generally dissipated above the ground so that keen-nosed game cannot detect human presence. However, a tree stand is no guarantee your scent won't reach the ground. Stands should be situated so prevailing winds will carry a hunter's scent away from the game trail or feeding area.
- Most game animals do not expect danger from above unless hunting pressure from tree stands is heavy. They are less aware of potential danger from above than at ground level, so they are less likely to see you.
- Movements and sounds that may be made in preparing for the shot are usually minimal; the chances of alerting game are slim.
- If undetected, the bowhunter in a tree frequently has the luxury of taking his time and selecting the best possible shot offered by the animal.

Of course, certain disadvantages do exist in tree stand hunting. Selecting the proper tree, positioning the stand at the best height and angle, and finding or creating adequate shooting lanes may be a puzzle or challenge to the beginner. Some bowhunters simply are not cut out for the sit-and-wait method where patience and confidence in their location are necessary ingredients for success. Finally, there is the possible danger of a fall. Safety belts or lines should always be used by tree stand hunters and care should be taken when climbing in and out of the stand, especially in cold or wet weather.

Tree stand hunting also requires more effort than taking a stand on the ground. Tree stands take time to set up. Commotion in setting up and accessing tree stands is often unavoidable. There can be considerable expense in buying portable tree stands.

Whenever possible, use suitable tree limbs or portable stands. Permanent tree stands are illegal in some areas and are eyesores everywhere. Nails can damage trees. Never erect any stand until you have the landowner's permission and check the laws in your hunting area. When cutting shooting lanes, keep all trimming of leaves and twigs or small limbs to an absolute minimum. Do this well in advance of the season, if possible, and remove all trimmings. Strap-on tree steps or blocks are ideal for getting up and down the tree. Never climb when carrying your bow; use a cord for raising and lowering equipment and hunting tackle.

Photo by Mike Strandlund

Many bowhunters make the mistake of failing to camouflage themselves in a tree stand. A hunter silhouetted against the sky is very easy for deer to see and avoid.

When positioning tree stands, keep the sun, wind, and direction of your approach and the animal's approach in mind. While a tree stand may prevent you from being scented, don't depend on it. Locate your stand where the prevailing winds (from the west in most regions) will blow your scent away from the animal's likely direction of approach. If possible, locate the stand between the sun and the animal's likely position—this will make it easier for you to see the animal and harder for the animal to see you. Set up the stand so you don't have to approach from a direction where the animal might detect you. And position it so you will be in a comfortable position to shoot where the animal will probably be standing.

Also keep shooting distances in mind. Some novice bowhunters make the mistake of setting up a tree stand directly over a trail, and find themselves with a difficult straight-down shot. The ideal shooting distance for most treestand hunters is 15 to 25 yards from the animal. Set up your stand accordingly.

Locate your tree stand near the junction of two or more well-used game trails. Stands overlooking feeding and watering areas, deer scrapes, elk wallows, and other game "funnels" may also prove effective. Always approach and enter your stand as quietly as possible to avoid alerting nearby game. Pay attention to where you step and don't walk where human scent can spook approaching animals. Never relieve yourself in the vicinity of your stand.

The height of effective tree stands varies greatly, from a low of eight feet to a high of 18 to 20 feet or more. The average is probably found somewhere between the two extremes; however, what's best for you will depend on several factors including the terrain, surroundings, prevailing winds, and species of game being hunted. Tree stand hunting may be successfully combined with baiting methods (if legal) and calling or attracting game by the use of scents or calls. Investigate the various options to improve your odds.

If you plan to hunt from a tree, practice shooting from elevated positions—preferably from the tree stand itself. Many bowhunters in trees tend to shoot high or over their intended target.

Ground Blind Hunting

Ground-level blinds—even pit blinds constructed partially below ground—are another effective means of bowhunting. The idea here is to locate your blind and conceal yourself near game trails or feeding areas where you expect game to pass or gather. The blind must keep you undetected by the game until you release your arrow.

You must realize that wind direction is of paramount importance to the bowhunter using a ground blind. Because your scent is on the same level as your quarry, it may be detected

Sitting quietly in a ground blind can be an excellent method of hunting under certain conditions, though it can be difficult to draw your bow without being seen.

easily. Also, most big game animals expect predators to attack from ground level, and will be especially alert to any unusual movements, sounds, or odors from the ground. Always keep noise and motion to an absolute minimum. This advice also holds true for entering and exiting ground blinds.

Like treestand hunting, you must position yourself correctly. If you're too close to a trail, you run a higher risk of detection. Too far, and shots are tougher. Twenty to 30 yards from the trail, feeding area, watering hole, or other place where you expect game to be is a good range in most cases.

The best blinds are natural blinds. Boulders, blowdowns, stumps—anything that will break the hunter's telltale silhouette—are good places if there is good game sign nearby. Build blinds ahead of the hunting season so game animals may become accustomed to these structures. Always obtain permission before erecting a blind and keep all cutting and trimming to a bare minimum. Disturb the surroundings as little as possible. Animals quickly notice changes in their home areas.

Generally, shooting lanes will be limited with only certain shots available to a bowhunter in a well-concealed ground blind. Consequently, you may not have the luxury of time in choosing the best possible shot. Visibility may also be limited.

Photo by Mike Strandlund

Since long periods of waiting for game to appear are more often the rule than the exception, comfort is essential. Standing, crouching and kneeling can tire you out within minutes, and if you're uncomfortable, you will tend to move more. A stool, log, or similar seat may be used; however, bowhunters using this method should practice shooting while seated. Camouflage is vital. Since you are eye-level with your quarry, keep all movements slow and deliberate. Jack-in-the-box, jump-up-and-shoot tactics rarely work for bowhunters.

An important part of hunting from stands is to clear shooting lanes. Twigs—even very small ones—will deflect an arrow off target.

Still-Hunting and Stalking

Still-hunting and stalking game is widely regarded as the most challenging method of bowhunting. It may be the most rewarding as well, because a hunter taking any big game animal with these methods has won the most difficult game in bowhunting.

A still-hunter moves through his hunting area very slowly and silently, doing at least three times as much looking and standing as walking. The idea here is to hunt into the wind and to spot your quarry before it sees you. When game is sighted, the still-hunter attempts to intercept or stalk closer to the animal, closing the distance and getting into position for a good shot.

Unlike the hunter who waits for the animal to approach his ambush site near a ground blind or tree stand, the still-hunter must move to the animal and remain undetected. With most big game species, this is no easy task. Not only must you keep tabs on the breeze; you must remain unseen and unheard as you work into position for the ideal shot.

The stalking hunter first spots his target animal, usually by careful glassing with binoculars. Then he plans a way to sneak up on the animal by remaining undetected until he gets into bow range. While this is no easy chore, it's usually easier than still-hunting, because the hunter has the advantage of knowing where the animal is.

Photos by Mike Strandlund

Stalking and still-hunting are the most challenging methods of bowhunting. Sneaking into bow range of a game animal takes great skill and patience.

When stalking or still-hunting, use every resource at hand to keep from being seen, scented, or heard. Try to stay out of sight of the animal until you raise to shoot. Use scent suppressors and cover scents, but always keep the wind in your favor. Some serious bowhunters remove their shoes when still-hunting or closing in on a stalk for the quietest possible walking. If you use this method, it's best to have an extra pair of heavy wool socks to protect your feet.

Good camouflage is a must for this type of hunting. All movements should be made in slow motion and never while the animal is looking in your direction. Avoid making undue noise and be alert for sudden shifts in wind direction.

For very wary game like the whitetail, still-hunting is the least productive of the basic bowhunting methods. It is better suited to game that displays duller wits or less caution—caribou, moose, and some mule deer.

Other Bowhunting Methods

Driving game, a method whereby a hunter or group of hunters attempts to push animals past waiting hunters, is sometimes a workable bowhunting method.

Photo by Mike Strandlund

Well-laid-out drives can often work well for bowhunting deer, elk, and some other game. Small pushes through thick cover can get inactive animals up and moving past standers, but good, high-percentage shots can be hard to come by.

The best locations for drives are small patches of dense cover in otherwise open areas. These include woodlots, small fields of standing corn, creekbottoms, and brushy mountain draws, among others. Game concentrates here, and it is easy to isolate these areas and coordinate members of the drive.

When setting up a drive, keep in mind that animals should be moved downwind or crosswind—never into the wind, or they will scent standers. Make drives in a way that tends to funnel animals through a few narrow escape routes, to make most efficient use of standers.

The biggest disadvantage of driving is that the game is often alarmed and offers only a running shot. Shots must be chosen well.

Bowhunting game from canoes or other types of boats, where legal, is an effective way to hunt certain big and small game species. Typically, boats are used by bowhunters as a means of transportation to remote areas or for bowfishing expeditions. But floating or paddling silently along inland waterways can be a viable bowhunting method.

Horseback hunting is another option and pack-in trips are common in some western states. Horses carry bowhunters and camping gear into backcountry hunting areas. Occasionally bowhunters will ride until game is sighted, dismount, and attempt to stalk within good bow range.

Backpack bowhunting has gained popularity in recent years. Carrying his camp, food, and hunting tackle, the bowhunter hikes into remote hunting areas in search of game. Once the animals are located, he usually employs still-hunting and stalking techniques or hunts from natural blinds.

When To Shoot

One of the most critical decisions you will make as a bowhunter is determining the precise moment to release an arrow. Often the success or failure of the hunt—perhaps an entire season—is judged by this single act. Therefore, all bowhunters should recognize the necessity of learning the best time to shoot.

On the surface, when to shoot may seem to be an easy decision for any hunter to make. "Take the first good shot you get" is typical advice passed along from veteran to beginning bowhunter. But what constitutes a *good shot*? You must keep in mind that each individual—and each hunting situation—is different. What's *good* for one person might be *risky* or *poor* to another. Learning when to shoot depends on a number of factors including personal shooting ability, hunting experience, distance and target position, personal ethics and proper equipment to name a few. The knowledge actually comes from within. In fact, only one person—you—can judge when the time is right to release.

Mental and physical preparedness is the key. You must realize that no conscientious bowhunter ever ventures afield without a thorough understanding of his hunting equipment, game laws and his personal proficiency.

Animal Position

It would be impossible to learn when to shoot without first understanding the importance of animal position and arrow placement. Even though these aspects are examined elsewhere in this manual, they cannot be overemphasized.

Usually, the best shot a bowhunter can take on deer-sized game is one when the animal is standing in a quartering away position. Next best is the classic broadside shot, preferably at a stationary or slowly moving target. It's best if the animal is fairly calm. Those that are alert and ready to spring are the

Photos by Gabby Barrus

Bowhunters are faced frequently with the dilemma of the marginal shot. Animals are often moving a little too fast, are a little too far, or are facing toward or away from you. It takes self discipline to do what must be done in these situations—pass up the shot.

113

animals most likely to "jump the string"—duck or bound from the path of the arrow when they hear the bow discharge.

Unfortunately, animals do not always cooperate with you or position themselves well. At such times all bowhunters must determine whether to wait for a better opportunity or to release their arrow. Keeping in mind that all risky shots should be avoided, there are several effective positions where a well-placed arrow will result in a quick, clean kill. There are also several shots that you should avoid under normal circumstances.

The head or neck shot may be an effective choice for the gun hunter, but no conscientious bowhunter should ever at-

Photo by Len Rue Jr.

The ideal bow shot—the animal is close, unalert, and a bit off-balance, with its near front leg a bit forward, making your angle to the vital zone bigger.

tempt such a marginal shot. The brain is a relatively small target surrounded by arrow-stopping bone. And while the neck offers several vital areas—spinal column, jugular vein and carotid artery—these too are relatively tiny targets well-hidden within a large area of non-vital muscle. Generally, fatal neck and brain shots by bowhunters are accidental hits where the sharp broadhead just happens to sever something vital. Avoid them!

Frontal shots may prove lethal providing the arrow penetrates into the heart-lung-liver area and does sufficient damage. But the chances of a poor hit are too great to warrant taking this shot under average conditions. The cardiovascular area is protected from the front by heavy bone structure. Shots, unless perfectly placed, may embed in the brisket, chest or shoulder area. The result may be a non-lethal hit and a lost animal. Another negative factor is that when an animal is facing you the chances are greater he is already alerted to your presence of will spot you at the instant of release and bolt. This greatly increases your chances of making a poor hit. Again, front-facing shots are seldom worth the risk involved.

Another questionable shot for the ground-level bowhunter is the animal that faces directly away and presents its rear to the shooter. An arrow that cuts the femoral artery on the inside of either hind leg will result in certain death. The same is true of the arrow that penetrates through to the animal's chest cavity. Even the shot that flies high could strike the spinal column in the animal's neck. But many bowhunters believe the rear-end shot is risky at best and avoid it. Heavy hip, pelvic and leg bones can impede arrow penetration and result in a non-fatal wound. Unquestionably, broadside and quartering-away shots are preferable.

The broadside shot is popular and offers the bowhunter the biggest target area; however, it is important to understand that concentration is necessary. A properly placed arrow will often slice through both lungs, the heart or liver—all fatal hits. But an arrow too far forward can embed itself in the shoulder bone and stop short of inflicting a mortal wound. Also, an arrow too far back can result in a dreaded paunch or intestinal hit. An arrow that hits high might miss the lungs and aortic artery, resulting in a sparse blood trail and a tough recovery job.

On big, tough game like moose, elk, or brown bear, where good penetration is especially important, most bowhunters prefer broadside shots over quartering away shots. This avoids the added difficulty of penetrating through the stomach to reach the vitals. An accurate broadside shot also ensures a double-lung hit, helping to bring down tough game quickly.

Beyond doubt, the most deadly bowhunting shot on deer-sized game occurs when the animal is facing away at a 45 degree angle. A broadhead angling forward behind the rib cage will miss ribs and travel a long route through the vitals. An animal standing in this position exposes virtually its entire vital zone and presents a large target.

Resist the temptation to shoot at running game unless you're well-practiced at that game or the animal is already wounded. Few bowhunters have the skill necessary to place their arrow in the kill area of a rapidly moving target.

The Vital Area

A bowhunter should shoot for one of three vital organs: the heart, lungs, or liver. Striking one of these with a sharp broadhead will lead to a quick kill.

A hit in the heart brings death quickly. But it is a small target. Because the heart is located just above the front leg bone, a shot a few inches low may hit this bone. A shot a few inches forward will likely hit the animal's upper leg bone, and a shot a few inches back will miss any vital organs. Do not aim for the heart. Rather, pick a spot higher and farther back on the chest cavity.

The lungs fill the front half of the main body cavity, inside the rib cage and behind and above the heart. A hit in the lungs will cause them to hemorrhage and collapse instantly. A solid double-lung hit results in a quick and humane death.

Also located in the front half of the body cavity is the liver, which filters blood. It is composed of many small blood vessels. A hit in the liver is almost always fatal. And, as with a heart and lung shot, the animal does not travel far after being hit. There is usually a good blood trail—especially with complete penetration and bleeding from two holes.

The area you want to aim for, however, should be the center of the lung, liver and heart area. Where is that spot? The International Bowhunter Education Program teaches a good rule of thumb to locate this spot. Disregard the head and neck of the deer and mentally pick the mid-point of the animal. Now move ahead about four inches and you've got it. Another way to locate this spot is to observe a deer standing broadside. Move your eye up the back side of the front leg to a point

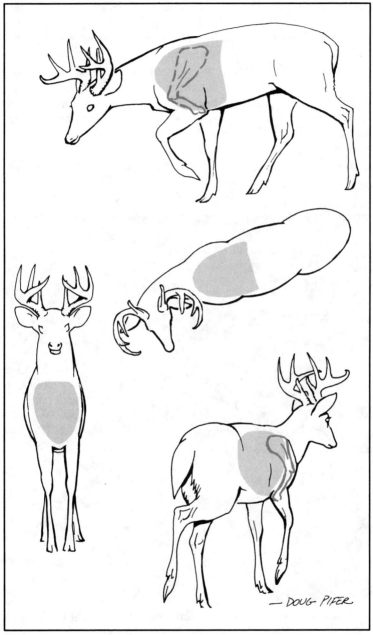

One of the keys to successful bowhunting is knowing where to shoot an animal. These illustrations show this vital area from broadside, above, quartering away, and head-on. Note how the shoulder blade and upper leg bone shield the vital zone at different angles.

117

one-half the way on the body cavity. That's it.

Once you've learned where that spot is, practice shooting at it. Keep in mind that perhaps the most common reason for missed shots is that the hunter does not concentrate on that one spot, mistakenly shooting at the whole deer. When practicing, try putting no target on the hay bales. Just mentally pick a spot, concentrate and shoot at this imaginary spot. Do the same with deer targets. Pick a single small spot on the target and try to hit it.

Remember, whether practicing or bowhunting, your first arrow is usually the most important one. Make it count because you may not get a second shot.

Photo by Linda Lou Steiner

Learning to bowhunt takes time and dedication. You'll have to put together your knowledge of your equipment, along with hunting and woodsmanship skills to become a successful bowhunter.

Education and Self Discipline

Learning to bowhunt takes time and dedication. Proper preparation is the key.

Knowledge of your equipment and its limitations is essential. You must also know yourself and your personal abilities. Books and articles will help, as will first-hand advice from experienced bowhunters and bowhunter education clinics. Study the type of animal you'll hunt, and analyze the best approach to hunting animals in your area. Practice under simulated hunting conditions and scout your hunting areas well ahead of opening day. Avoid any shot beyond your effective shooting range.

Bowhunters, perhaps more than other types of hunters, learn from their experiences—failures as well as successes. The thoroughly prepared bowhunter who looks on each trip afield as a learning experience as well as an adventure is already well along the road to bowhunting success.

CHAPTER 7

BOWHUNTING BIG GAME

Mention bowhunting to most people and they'll immediately think of deer hunting. Deer are the only species of big game found in every state and province. Regardless of where you live, deer hunting—for whitetails, mule deer, or blacktails—is generally possible close to home with a minimum investment of time and money. They offer

Photo by Richard P. Smith

The challenge of going after big game with a bow, and the exhilaration and satisfaction that comes with success, is unsurpassed in the sporting world.

bowhunting's best opportunities, and perhaps its biggest challenge.

Bowhunters accept the challenge of hunting deer and other big game for a variety of reasons. Once they've learned the basics of shooting a bow and arrow, they often turn full attention to taking their first deer. And once deer hunting becomes routine, they broaden their bowhunting horizons by seeking black bears, pronghorn, elk, caribou, or any of the other North American big game species commonly pursued by serious bowhunters.

It's not unusual for people living east of the Mississippi to dream of a western bowhunt just as people in the West often look to Canada or Alaska as the site of their dream hunt. Some bowhunting addicts even look abroad—to game-rich Africa and beyond—for adventure with the hunting bow.

Years ago bowhunting was a seasonal sport, generally limited to the fall deer seasons. No more. Now you and a legion of camouflaged bow and arrow enthusiasts may legally pursue game animals every month of the year. Long archery seasons and ample bag limits are the norm. Air travel has made our modern world smaller and remote areas are easier to access. Your hunting adventures are limited only by the time and money you want to spend.

Matching Methods to the Game

Whether you travel widely in pursuit of a variety of game or stay close to home and focus full attention on nearby deer, you can know the challenges of bowhunting and experience the thrill of the hunt. Bowhunters have successfully hunted every species of North American big game using the techniques mentioned in the previous chapter. In the following pages you will find an overview of the many opportunities awaiting modern-day big game bowhunters along with general tips on successful bowhunting techniques.

Whitetail Deer

The whitetail deer is the undisputed number-one big game animal in North America. Abundant, adaptable, wily, and challenging, beautiful and prized both as trophy and tablefare, America's whitetail deer are found throughout the continent from Canada to Mexico and in all contiguous states. All but Nevada, Utah, and California have huntable numbers of the animals.

Bowhunters bag more whitetails each season than any other species. Nationwide, the whitetail success rate averages about 12 percent for bowhunters. Most deer are shot by bowhunters who sit quietly in a tree stand. Surveys show that most successful shots are made at less than 20 yards from tree stands overlooking trails, field edges, oak or apple groves, or scrapes.

Photo by Richard P. Smith

The whitetail deer is by far the most abundant and sought-after big game animal by bowhunters.

While hunting from elevated stands is undoubtedly the most effective way to collect your venison, you may wish to attempt still-hunting and stalking. This is a challenging test of any bowhunter's skills, since a deer's senses are exceptional and moving into good bow range of a whitetail is very hard to do. Deer typically rely on their noses and ears more than their eyes to warn of danger. While a whitetail tends to overlook a camouflaged, motionless hunter, movement of any kind is likely to draw immediate attention.

Regardless, each season some bowhunters readily accept the challenge of still-hunting—easing into whitetail cover and slipping quietly and slowly into the wind. A handful succeed at intercepting or encountering unwary deer. The key is seeing

123

game first and then moving carefully or simply waiting until a shot presents itself.

While stalking and still-hunting deer at ground level can work, most bowhunters who don't hunt from trees prefer to adopt a sit-and-wait approach. Natural or man-made blinds near travel routes, waterholes, and feeding areas can pay dividends for any patient hunter willing to invest the necessary time waiting for deer to appear.

The deer drive, popular in many gun-hunting circles, can work for bowhunters, but is not an ideal bowhunting technique since most animals will be alarmed, alert, and moving. Deer in such situations are difficult targets.

The annual fall breeding period, or rut, is a time when the largely solitary bucks seek out does and lose some of their normal wariness. Many trophy hunters concentrate on this brief period as the best time to take an exceptional animal. As the rutting frenzy progresses, bucks may be seen at any time of day. They disdain normal feeding and bedding activity, traveling all day and breeding as many does as they can. Scrapes—pawed areas where bucks leave their scent—are checked and freshened by the far-ranging whitetail bucks.

Antler rattling and calling are two hunting methods used by many successful bowhunters prior to, during, and immediately after the rut. "Horn rattling" simulates the sounds of rival bucks fighting and may attract curious bucks or does to the site of the staged battle. Also, whitetails occasionally communicate by bleating and grunting. Callers able to reproduce such sounds may attract deer.

Some serious bowhunters employ a combination of reliable, time-tested techniques with innovations involving scents, calls, and even deer decoys. Food and sex scents are capable of luring deer close to a waiting hunter while masking scents are designed to confuse a whitetail's keen sense of smell. Calls that pique a deer's curiosity and decoys that visually attract deer may be used successfully in combination with various scent products.

Many archery deer seasons begin prior to the main period of the breeding season or rut; therefore, locating fresh rubs and scrapes to find a buck's territory is not possible then. Besides, you'll probably do your scouting long before rutting begins. What then should you look for? Food and cover are extremely important to deer all year, and are important factors in helping you find deer prior to deer season.

Look for deer trails, droppings, and tracks. A good time to look for fresh trails is during spring, right after snow melts. At this time the ground is wet, rains are common, and deer trails to and from feeding areas are relatively easy to see. Keep in mind that this scouting is best suited to locating deer and seeing where they concentrate—feeding habits will probably change by the time hunting season arrives, and so will deer patterns.

Locating Deer

Feeding areas are not difficult to find in summer and early fall, especially in areas where forests are interspersed with farm fields. Although most hunters have come to believe that deer spend most of their time consuming woody twigs, this is not true in the early season. Deer spend more time grazing

Photos by Richard P. Smith

Expert bowhunters study the signs deer leave to determine where they are concentrating. Favored food sources and travel routes, indicated by marks in ground and vegetation, are among the best places to hunt.

than browsing; they probably spend more time feeding at ground level than they do at twig level.

Foods found on the ground such as waste corn, alfalfa, soybeans, grasses, acorns, apples (wild and domestic), persimmons, forbes, and mushrooms are common diet items. Look for a mixture of these foods when looking for a good deer area. Feeding sign may be difficult to discern at first. Acorns cut in half, as if by knife, are a good sign. So are sumac stems, trimmed about six to twelve inches from the ground, along the edge of a field. The browsing sign of deer differs from that of rabbits; deer leave ragged ends on twigs while rabbits bite them off cleanly.

When positioning your blind, remember that although you saw deer in the area before the season, you won't necessarily see them when the season opens. The feeding patterns of deer change from season to season. Also, deer enter fields much later as the fall season progresses. Thus, if you see feeding sign in a field during the season, position your stand along an active trail or at the intersection of two ridge trails leading into the field. You may wish to be 200-300 yards from the field, so that a deer timing its travel to reach the field at nightfall will pass your stand in shooting light.

When hunting in the morning, be at your stand at least a half-hour before daylight, when deer move to bedding areas. Be there three to four hours before nightfall, when they move toward feeding areas.

Note the wind when placing your stand in the thicket. A basic rule to remember is that before daylight, cool air prevails and moves downhill into the ravines and fields at the foot of mountains. As the sun comes up, the air warms and rises, moving uphill toward the ridges. Thus, in the evening, as deer move down from bedding areas, they walk into the wind until the sun sets and the air cools. Position your stand accordingly. For example, if your stand is close to the edge of a field, and the deer enter the field early, you must guard against your scent moving uphill with the warm air current.

Buck Rubs and Scrapes

Deer hunting during the rut offers a bowhunter a better chance of success because whitetail bucks let down their defenses during mating season. They also leave evidence of their travel patterns—which can show a hunter where best to take a stand—in the form of rubs and scrapes.

Buck rubs—small trees rubbed bare of bark two to four feet off the ground—are a sure sign of bucks. Most buck rubs, however, are not made by deer attempting to remove velvet. Most whitetail rubs are made in October and November as a part of the mating ritual. Rubs are made as bucks vent hormonal frustrations and are also a form of communication between bucks.

A large buck tends to make large rubs on larger trees. When you find large buck rubs you are in a good hunting area, though a rub is not always a prime stand location.

Scrapes are made by bucks during the rut, both in normal day-to-day activities and when they are ready to breed does. A scrape is a pawed area of bare ground made by the hooves of the buck. They can look like turkey scratchings, but turkeys usually scratch throughout an area. A buck scrape is much more localized.

Photo by Joann Kirk

Whitetail bucks make scrapes on the ground to delineate territories and mark breeding areas. Scrapes that are renewed regularly and are large or among several in a line make good stand sites.

A scrape location may or may not be a good place to locate a stand. There are some basic rules to follow when looking for active scrapes that would make good stand sites. Select large, singular scrapes that are located on the same spot in successive years, scrapes with urine odor, scrapes located at the hub of incoming deer trails (the more the better) and scrapes with a small overhanging branch or twig broken off by the buck. When hunting near scrapes, remember to position your stand relative to air currents. Keep human odor to a minimum.

Whitetails currently number upwards of 20 million animals and continue to expand their range annually. Over 30 sub-species are recognized and one—the Coues deer of the south-western U.S. and Mexico—is recognized as a separate big game trophy category by both the Pope and Young Club and Boone and Crockett Club. Because of their tendency to range widely over open country, Coues deer are generally hunted by glassing and stalking.

For more details on whitetail behavior and methods of hunting them, get the NRA Hunter Skills Series book, *Whitetail Deer Hunting*.

NRA Staff Photos

While most whitetails are taken by trail-watching from a stand, more and more bowhunters are finding success with more exciting methods, such as attracting deer with calling, rattling, scents and decoys.

Black Bears

If the whitetail deer is bowhunting's reigning monarch, the black bear is certainly the prince of North American big game. The Pope and Young Club records show black bears and pronghorn antelope running a close race for the second place spot for total trophy entries.

Black bears are found in greatest numbers in Alaska and Canada, although a huntable population ranges across much of the United States. Throughout much of the Rocky Mountain range, color variations are common, with cinnamon brown, red, and blond the most typical shades.

Bears travel widely in a continuous search for food. They are solitary animals, although sows and cubs may remain together for two years. Breeding occurs during the summer

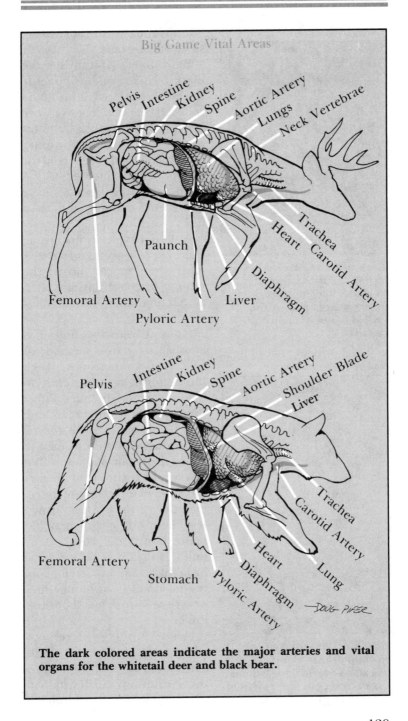

Big Game Vital Areas

Pelvis Intestine Kidney Spine Aortic Artery Lungs Neck Vertebrae

Paunch

Trachea Heart Carotid Artery

Diaphragm

Femoral Artery Liver

Pyloric Artery

Pelvis Intestine Kidney Spine Aortic Artery Shoulder Blade Liver

Trachea Carotid Artery

Femoral Artery Heart Lung

Stomach Diaphragm

Pyloric Artery

DOUG PIFER

The dark colored areas indicate the major arteries and vital organs for the whitetail deer and black bear.

Black bears are probably the second-favorite target of bowhunters. Their range covers a large part of the United States and most of Canada.

Most black bears taken by bowhunters are shot from a tree stand overlooking bait that has been set out and revisited periodically by bears.

months and cubs are born in the sows' winter dens.

Bowhunters typically use the black bear's ravenous appetite as the most effective means to collect a bearskin trophy. More black bears are taken by hunting over bait than by any other hunting method. Tree stands or ground blinds situated within good shooting range have proved the undoing of many a hungry bruin.

Although typically nocturnal, black bears in search of an easy meal often appear during the waning hours of daylight. It is at that time bait hunting is most effective.

Hunting bears with hounds is another effective method of collecting your trophy. Such hunts normally begin early in the day when hunters range through bear country searching for fresh sign. Keen-scented strike dogs—hounds trained to locate the spoor of game—find tracks and sort out the bruin's direction of travel before the remainder of the pack is turned in. These dog chases may last many hours and cover many miles. If the bruin refuses to be brought to bay in a tree or on the ground, a bowhunter may never see—much less shoot at—the bear.

Hound hunting is a respected, centuries-old sport with the excitement of the chase holding the greatest appeal for its participants. Keeping within hearing distance of the dogs while negotiating brushy swamps or high-country canyons can be among the most physically demanding types of hunting. The shot—if and when it is made—is often considered anticlimactic, and most bears taken with the assistance of hounds are hard-earned and well-deserved big game trophies.

In many areas of the West, where public land is plentiful and logging operations have opened forested slopes, bowhunters often try glassing feeding areas in an attempt to locate bears busy filling their stomachs. Animals sighted may then be stalked if conditions permit.

Bears have relatively poor eyesight; however, their senses of smell and hearing are among the most acute in the animal world. Slipping undetected within bow range of a bear is a true stalking challenge.

A few bowhunters have had success calling bears to them by imitating the distress call of fawns or rabbits. Curious and ever-hungry, the bears that respond offer a challenging target to waiting hunters. Such bruins are alert, expecting an easy meal, and quick to detect movement of any kind. Called-in bears usually present a head-on, frontal shot that is risky for archery tackle; however, a patient bowhunter may be able to avoid being seen and get an ideal broadside or quartering-away shot as the bear moves past.

Finally, a few bears are bagged each year by opportunistic bowhunters in search of other game such as deer, elk, or caribou. In parts of the country where ranges of various species overlap, buying an extra license or game tag may prove to be a wise investment.

Western Big Game

Mule deer and blacktails, elk, antelope, cougar, bighorn sheep, and mountain goat are the game animals most commonly hunted across the western regions of North America.

Mule Deer

While whitetails are brush-loving animals of the forest fringes, mule deer typically haunt rather open terrain where they depend more on their eyesight than smell to detect danger. They also range much farther across their home range and tend to be more gregarious than whitetails.

Because these deer can be difficult to pattern, bowhunting mule deer from tree stands is not as effective or as widely

The vast landscapes of the American West provide a spectacular hunting environment, but the mountains and wide open spaces can present serious problems in getting into bow range of big game.

practiced. Regardless, elevated stands—especially those placed near trails leading to feeding and watering areas or natural mineral licks—can and do account for numerous deer each year. But without question most mule deer are taken by bowhunters who still-hunt and stalk animals they've sighted from a distance. During the rut, mule deer bucks may be lured within bow range by rattling.

Mule deer are considerably easier to still-hunt and stalk than whitetails, especially under the cover of aspen forest and sagebrush. Does and smaller bucks may sometimes regard an approaching hunter with more curiosity than fright.

A typical method for bowhunting mule deer is to glass open areas at first light, trying to locate the deer you want. Then stalk the animal, or stalk to a location you've plotted where you have a good chance of intercepting the deer.

In the middle of the day, the most productive methods are still-hunting good bedding areas, or glassing and stalking muleys that are bedded under scarce trees in otherwise open areas. Carefully driving small patches of cover, trying to move deer without scaring them into a long run, is also productive. Muleys pushed out of cover without being too frightened are apt to hesitate and look back at drivers while in range of a well-placed stander.

Blacktail deer are one of 11 mule deer subspecies. They range from Canada south along coastal areas to California and

With bigger antlers and less wariness than a whitetail, mule deer are favorite targets of bowhunters. They are difficult to pattern, however, and stalking is often the only hope of getting within range.

typically prefer thick cover over open country. A blacktail buck is usually lighter with notably smaller antlers than muleys. Bowhunting techniques that take whitetails also work well for blacktails.

Elk

Two of six subspecies of elk—Rocky Mountain or Yellowstone elk and Roosevelt elk—are commonly sought by bowhunters each fall. The former species is widely distributed from Canada to the American Southwest, with transplanted herds found as far east as Michigan. Roosevelt elk are found in British Columbia, Washington, and Oregon, with some transplanted herds living on islands off the Alaskan Coast. Roosevelts are the largest elk, but these bulls usually lack the impressive antlers of their Rocky Mountain brethren.

The most popular elk hunting method is bugling during the fall rut when bulls seek to gather harems of cows and challenge each other for breeding dominance. Calling lovesick bulls with cow calls or challenging bulls with bugles can result in shots.

Photo by Gabby Barrus

The regal bull elk is the most coveted trophy of American bowhunters. Once an animal of the plains and eastern woodlands, it now inhabits the most difficult terrain of the West.

Stand hunting at waterholes, food plots, or wallows also works, and still-hunting accounts for other shooting opportunities each season. Elk rely primarily on their sense of smell and do not hesitate to move into new areas when hunting pressure disturbs them.

Pronghorn

Pronghorn, or antelope, are animals of the open prairies, where their keen eyesight and speed keep them safe from predators. Although stalking pronghorns in areas of rolling or broken terrain is possible, most successful shots are made by bowhunters waiting in blinds near waterholes. In the dry country typical of most antelope habitat, watering sites are scarce and frequented by livestock and game animals alike. A patient hunter, carefully concealed downwind from a spring, stock tank, or pond, can often get close-range shots impossible under other hunting conditions. Decoying pronghorns has become increasingly popular in recent years and can be an especially effective technique during the rut. A few bowhunters

134

Photo by Gerald A. Almy

A boon to elk bowhunters is that hunting seasons coincide with the breeding season. Rutting bulls respond to bugling and cow calling, often bugling in response to betray their location or occasionally approaching the caller.

Photo by Jim Zumbo

Bowhunters seeking the keen-sighted pronghorn usually take a stand at waterholes, fence crossings or in the lofty perch of a windmill.

combine decoying with calling. Although few tree stand sites exist in antelope country, hunting from elevated stands—a windmill or a haystack, for example—works well.

135

Cougar

Cougar, or mountain lion hunting is usually trailing in snow with a good pack of hounds equally adept at running bears and cats. Only a handful of lions have ever been killed by bowhunters without the assistance of dogs. This is due in part

Photo by Leonard Lee Rue III

Photo by Gabby Barrus

Two other western big game animals pursued by bowhunters are the cougar and Rocky Mountain bighorn sheep. These trophies are hard to come by, due to limited permits available, rugged terrain, and the demanding hunting methods required.

to the remote country occupied by the shy, secretive big cats, which are usually nocturnal hunters. A few hunters' lions have responded to predator calls, but calling cougars is not widely practiced. The cats travel widely across a large home range and prey mainly on deer. Fresh lion kills are prized by houndsmen as ideal starting points for their pack to take up the scent. Cougars often remain near their kills after feeding and may return to the carcass from time to time.

Bighorn Sheep

Bighorn sheep are highly prized bowhunting trophies, among the most difficult to obtain. The rugged, desolate country sheep inhabit presents physical challenges to any hunter, and a sheep's exceptional eyesight makes approach within bow range no easy task.

Rocky Mountain bighorns are found in Rocky Mountain regions from the U.S. north into Canada. Desert bighorns are smaller than their cousins, with a home area restricted to southwestern states and northern Mexico.

Most hunting is done by glassing and stalking. A few rams are taken each season by bowhunters waiting near mineral licks, water, and other areas frequented by bighorns.

Mountain Goat

The pure white, black-horned mountain goat is at home on high mountain slopes well above timberline where few predators venture. Mountain goats are found in the northwestern United States, but are most common in Alaska, British Columbia, and Alberta.

Goats have good vision and climb to avoid danger, venturing into vertical terrain. Bowhunters locate feeding or bedded goats and attempt to stalk within arrow range without being seen, heard, or scented. The sheer cliffs, dizzying heights, and rugged rock formations of most goat ranges deter all but the most determined and physically fit bowhunters; however, those willing to tackle the challenge of goat hunting claim it is a unique hunting experience well worth the effort.

Northern Big Game

This continent's north country holds a great abundance of big game. It includes the largest bears—the grizzly and Alaskan brown bear—along with several varieties of moose and caribou, Dall and Stone sheep, and remnants of the prehistoric past—bison and muskoxen.

Northern big game is very big game. The animals have evolved to large size in comparison with their cousins down south as a means of conserving body heat. Their bones and muscles are massive and their hides are thick, posing a true challenge to a hunter trying to push an arrow through to the vitals. Heavy bows, strong, tough hunting heads, and precise arrow placement is most important for the bowhunter of northern big game.

Big Bears

Grizzly and brown bears are actually the same species, with only their size and home range separating them. Brown bears are animals of the Alaskan coast and offshore islands where their diet of fish enables them to grow much larger than grizzlies of the continent's interior. Large, powerful, and dangerous, the huge hump-shouldered bears are very difficult to bring down with an arrow and are sought by relatively few bowhunters. Bait hunting, now a generally illegal method of hunting these bruins, has accounted for many of the animals listed in the Pope and Young records. Today bow and arrow hunters typically use the glass-and-stalk method of easing into range of bears seen feeding or moving at a distance. Most bowhunters who hunt brown or grizzly bears do so only with large-caliber firearms backing them.

Brown bears share a number of islands with the diminutive Sitka blacktail deer of the Alaskan/Canadian coastal areas. Each year there are reports of confrontations between bears and deer hunters. There is some evidence to support the theory that some bears actually respond to deer calls and to rifle shots, apparently seeking an easy meal. Brown bears are quick to scent, find, and claim wounded animals, and some have raided meat poles near hunting camps. Bowhunters still-hunting and stalking Sitka deer must be constantly alert for bears. Blood trailing, calling, and packing or storing meat requires caution and common sense. No bowhunter should ever risk a confrontation with an angry brown bear.

Moose

The moose is the largest member of the deer family. The Alaska-Yukon moose is the biggest moose subspecies, growing tremendous palmated antlers highly prized by trophy hunters. The Canadian moose is somewhat smaller than his northern cousins, and is common throughout Canada and certain bordering states. The Shiras or Wyoming moose is the smallest

North American moose and is found in Rocky Mountain areas of the American West.

Moose have only fair eyesight but excellent hearing and olfactory abilities, traits that make stalking the big animals more difficult than many imagine. Where terrain permits, glassing willow flats and lake shores or waterways is one effective

Photo by Karl Maslowski

Photo by Stan Warren

Hunting northern big game — including moose and caribou — represents significant expense and long-distance travel for most bowhunters, but the size of the land and game make for exciting memories.

method of locating moose prior to a stalk. Still-hunting is practiced by some moose hunters, and drift hunting from canoe or raft can be effective. Each year a few moose are shot by hunters in tree stands strategically placed along travel routes. Calling bulls during the fall rut can tempt lovesick moose within good bow range of a concealed hunter. At times calling is combined with drift hunting through prime moose habitat with excellent results.

Caribou

Caribou have become a favorite target of bowhunters, and with good reason. The antlers of a bull are among the most impressive of all big game trophies; caribou can be found in great abundance at the right time and place, and are comparatively easy to approach within bow range.

Four types of caribou are recognized by the Pope and Young Club. These include mountain caribou, the darkest subspecies; barren ground caribou, animals of the arctic tundra; woodland caribou, the smallest subspecies and found only in Newfoundland and the Maritime Provinces; and the Quebec-Labrador caribou. Gregarious, migratory animals, caribou range widely and have little contact with man. They have a keen sense of smell and good eyesight although, like most animals, often fail to recognize stationary objects even at close ranges. Still-hunting and stalking account for most bowhunting success each year, although blinds established near river crossings or well-used travel routes can be deadly.

Thinhorn Sheep

The high country of this continent's desolate northlands is home to the Dall and Stone thinhorn sheep. The pure white Dall ranges throughout much of Alaska and western Canada while the darker Stone is limited to the Yukon and British Columbia. Like the bighorn sheep of the American West, thinhorns have exceptional vision. They live in rugged mountain country well above treeline where only the most determined, physically fit hunters ever go. Glassing and stalking account for most of the thinhorns tagged by bowhunters.

Muskoxen and Bison

Muskoxen and the American bison are two north country species that attract occasional attention of bowhunters. Muskox hunting typically is limited to guided hunts made by snow machine in frozen arctic wastelands. Herds are located and approached on foot. The animals form defensive circles or lines with bulls protecting the smaller members of the group. Shots are made as the bulls stand defiantly guarding the herd or as they begin to move off.

Hunting of the continent's last free-ranging bison herds is now limited to parts of Alaska, Canada, and Utah's Henry Mountains. Special drawings for licenses are held regularly, but to date only very few bowhunters have filled bison tags. Wild bison are generally hard to locate and difficult to approach. Considerable patience and stalking skill are needed to get within shooting distance of the big beasts.

Bowhunters have successfully hunted every species of North American big game. A hunting bow, in the hands of a competent individual, is very effective and a well-placed hunting arrow tipped with a razor-sharp broadhead is capable of quickly and humanely felling any animal.

Recovering Game

Once you have shot a game animal you owe that animal every possible effort to recover it. You also owe it to yourself to track down all wounded game. You owe it to the landowner and the general public as well. Every unrecovered animal left in the woods provides ammunition to those opposed to hunting. It also provides a landowner with a reason to post his property to you and other bowhunters in the future. An ethical bowhunter makes every possible effort to recover his game.

Following are methods that will increase your chances of recovering the animals you shoot. This section is written with deer as a reference because that species is commonly hunted and the comments can be applied to any big game animal.

After The Shot

"I've shot a deer. Now what?"

Once you've shot a deer, you must remain as calm as possible and do three basic things immediately.

First, mentally mark the exact spot the deer stood when you shot. This is where you will look for your arrow and signs of a hit such as hair and blood.

Second, watch the exact path of the deer as it leaves the area. Use trees, stumps, rocks, etc. as landmarks and visually trace the exact path of the deer. Be certain these markers are vividly impressed upon your mind and, if you are shooting from a tree stand, remember that things tend to look different from ground level. Make sure you positively identify the last

Recovering your animal after the shot is a responsibility of every bowhunter. Learn to read the signs, including cut hair and material found on the arrow.

spot you saw the deer, perhaps using a compass to take a reading on this visually-marked spot.

Third, remain totally quiet once you've shot an animal. Do not shout or call to a friend. Listen. If the deer falls nearby, you may hear it go down, or you may hear it cough. Also, if the animal changes direction once out of sight, you may hear that. Finally, there is another reason to remain quiet. If you were hunting from a tree stand, there's a good chance the deer may not realize that a human was present in the area. The human voice is an alarm signal to deer and might prompt an animal wounded in a semivital area to run for hundreds of yards before bedding or dropping, making it more difficult to find.

Give wounded animals every opportunity to lie down or drop near the point of the hit. This will often happen if the animal does not realize a human is present. Always remain quiet after you shoot and also while trailing.

How long should you wait before following the blood trail? Every situation is different; however, in general, you should wait about 30 minutes in your stand. If the deer is mortally wounded, it will probably lie down and die in a few minutes. If it senses you approaching, it may move far and fast before expiring, leaving a trail so sparse it is difficult to follow. If you wait too long, however, the blood trail could dry up or wash away, depending on conditions, and being able to rest could give a marginally hit deer a chance for recovery.

Move very quietly to the spot where the deer stood when shot. You may already have some idea of where the arrow struck, especially if you used brightly-colored fletching and/or nocks. If you've learned the types, lengths, and colors of hair from the different parts of the animal's body, you may be able to identify the location of the hit when you don't see where the arrow strikes. The appearance of the blood will also indicate the location of the hit. Bright red blood usually means an artery was cut. Light-colored blood containing bubbles means a lung shot. Dark blood indicates a kidney or liver shot. If there is watery blood and other matter at the site, it could have been a shot in the paunch.

Try to find the arrow at the point you shot. It may have passed completely through the deer, and can provide clues to how well the deer was hit. Then again, it may have missed. More than one bowhunter has sworn he had a vital hit only to discover later his arrow missed the animal entirely. If you think you missed the deer but cannot find the arrow, assume that you have a hit and attempt to find and follow the trail.

Blood Trailing

Once the arrow is found, examine it closely and also comb the nearby area. Bright blood is a good sign but you can also get bright blood from a superficial skin or front leg hit. If you find greenish material or dark matter on the shaft or ground, you have a gut or paunch shot. Such a hit is often a mortal wound but you must wait at least four hours—preferably six— before following the trail. This is true even if it is raining quite hard. If you have trouble following the trail, enlist the help of some friends and conduct a systematic search of the area.

Before starting to trail the deer, mark the point of the hit with tissue paper or some other type of marker. If you find blood immediately and feel that the hit was in the vital lung/ liver/heart area, then begin to follow the trail carefully. However, if you jump the deer from a bed within 100 to 150 yards, immediately abandon the search and wait another four to six hours, so long as the blood trail is not likely to dry up or wash away.

If you choose to get help in trailing your deer, remember that a maximum of three people should be used for following the blood trail. Any more "help" may obliterate the trail before you have a chance to follow it.

Have one person remain at the last spot blood was found while you and a companion pursue the trail. Never walk directly on the blood trail and remember to look ahead and behind to get a feel for where the animal may be headed. Often you can see the path of the animal without having a blood trail to follow.

Photo by Richard P. Smith

If you have difficulty trailing your animal, enlist some expert assistance. Following a sparse blood trail is surprisingly easy at night with a lantern, which makes blood drops "glow."

Place markers at small blood drops along the trail as you go. This makes it easy to backtrack to the last spot and begin searching again in cases where you lose the trail. Watch for blood on leaves (on the undersides as well as on top), on rocks, trees, etc. Look for broken twigs, bent grass, fresh tracks or disturbed leaves. Stalk the blood trail. Do not be fooled by the amount of blood on the ground. Some mortal hits may leave little blood, especially when you do not get complete penetration from a tree stand shot. This is because blood fills the body cavity but very little escapes from the entry hole. Some superficial hits—like a front leg shot—may leave a heavy blood trail that eventually peters out, and the animal fully recovers.

If You Lose The Trail

If you lose blood sign, get down on your hands and knees and search for the smallest trace of blood. If after searching diligently in this manner you still do not find the trail, follow the tracks or the trail in the direction the deer was moving when the last blood sign was found. It is possible bleeding may stop for a short time and then begin again. You may pick up further blood sign on down the trail.

Chances are you can find your deer if the arrow was well-placed. But if you do not find the animal and reach the end of all sign, get as many friends as you can and conduct an extensive search of the area. Working in ever-expanding circles is a good method. Follow the general direction the animal was heading but be aware that wounded game may double back. Check along any streams, rivers, ponds, or canals in the area. Check out hiding spots such as thickets and deadfalls. Follow likely trails. Watch for broken twigs or limbs, skid marks, turned leaves, tracks, and other evidence. If legal, you can use dogs to help trail the deer or search for the carcass.

What if it is raining? Location of the hit as well as the severity of the rain are important factors here. If you have a lung/liver/heart hit in heavy rain, you should pick up the trail immediately, following slowly and quietly. But if you have a paunch hit, you should sneak out of the woods and wait approximately six hours. The reasoning here is simply that the effects of the rain will be minimal since a paunch shot normally leaves little blood; you probably wouldn't be able to blood-trail the deer anyway. Also, if left undisturbed the deer may bed down within 100-150 yards and give you a good chance to locate and recover it after waiting, even with heavy rain.

All of what has already been said also applies to hits made before darkness sets in. If the hit is good, follow the trail; if it's not a good hit, wait as outlined above. Return to the woods with a pump-up gasoline or kerosene lantern. These lanterns give much better light than flashlights and make the blood trail much more visible. Have two lanterns, if possible, leaving one to mark the last blood sign. If you jump the deer from a bed, leave and return at first light in the morning.

Demonstrate respect for the game by making every effort to recover all animals, even if the sign looks minimal. If you've followed a light blood trail for a half-mile or more and the animal has not bedded, chances are the wound is superficial and the deer will recover. If you found the arrow and got less than three inches of penetration, the same is true. Arrow wounds are such that they heal rapidly with little or no aftereffects to the animals.

Rather than take a chance on wounding and losing an animal, pass up chancy shots and concentrate on placing your arrow in the vitals.

Field Care of Game

Once your animal is down and tagged, it's time to turn attention to proper field care of the game. No matter how large or small, game animals require essentially the same basic field-dressing steps and equipment.

First, we need to dispel a couple of common myths involving proper meat care. There is no need to cut an animal's throat to "bleed" the carcass. Arrows kill by hemorrhage, effectively draining the body of its blood or causing blood to collect in the chest cavity where it is easily removed along with the entrails. All a cut to the throat does is damage a cape and cause additional work for your taxidermist. Even if the hide is not being saved for tanning or mounting, the cut provides another opening for pesky flies or exposes meat to dust, dirt, and hair.

It is also best to leave the scent glands alone. Many old-time deer hunters advocate slicing these glands off the rear legs of their animals; however, touching them with fingers or knife and then handling or cutting the meat does more harm than good.

If possible, position the animal on its back or side in a shady, gently sloping area with the head higher than the body. A hunting buddy can help steady the animal or, if you're alone, you can use cord or twine to tie the legs out of the way. Next, take your sharp knife and make a shallow cut along one side of the penis and scrotum or the udder. Local laws may require that genitals remain on the dressed carcass; otherwise, remove the sex organs.

Straddling the animal, insert your knife (cutting side up) under the skin and cut all the way up to the breastbone. Take care to avoid slicing the intestines or stomach and to prevent cut hair from getting into the body cavity. With practice you can learn to use two fingers on either side of the knife, cutting with the sharp edge upward, to hold the viscera away from the blade as an incision is made.

Use a meat saw or your knife to cut through the rib cage to the brisket. The sternum is comprised of tough cartilage and additional pressure will be required.

146

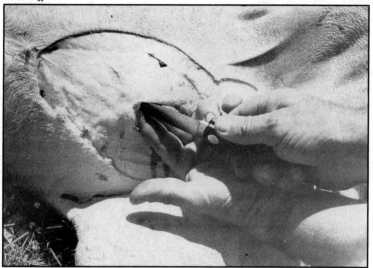

Be careful to avoid slicing the intestines and stomach when making your first incision. Cutting upward will prevent hair from getting in the chest cavity.

If the animal is an antlered or horned species and you want to preserve your trophy through taxidermy, do not cut into the neck above the animal's brisket. It's possible to ruin a cape or to incur additional taxidermy expense by needless cutting. A shoulder mount requires an incision up the back of the neck to the base of the skull. However, if the trophy is a fanged species and a rug mount planned, you may extend the cut all the way to the lower jaw. The same cut may be made on any species not bound for the taxidermist's studio.

Next, turn your attention to the other end of the animal and use your knife point to cut completely around the anus. Penetrate the pelvic cavity with the blade as you circle the vent. Pull the rectum away from the carcass and tie the vent closed with a piece of twine to prevent waste from being forced out during removal of the entrails. Next, use your saw to cut through the pelvic arch. Although a practiced hunter can accomplish the job with his knife, a saw or small axe is easier for the average person to use. After the cut is made, force both legs down until you hear the snap that signals a pelvic split.

Before attempting to remove the innards, you must cut the diaphragm free and loosen connecting tissue as required. Then, by cutting the windpipe and pulling it downward, you

To field-dress a big game animal, first (1) remove the sex organs if your animal is a male. (2) Cut through the belly hide and sternum, up to the animal's neck. (3) Finish the belly cut to the anus, split the pelvis bone, and cut out the colon. (4) Turn the body to one side and make any more cuts necessary to spill the paunch.

can start the evisceration process. You'll need to make additional cuts by reaching inside the animal and freeing connective tissue. Be especially careful with the bladder as you reach the pelvic area. A careless slip of the knife can result in urine leaking into the lower body cavity. However, if you've propped up the animal's front end and done the job properly, all internal organs and intestines will spill out neatly between the animal's back legs.

The heart and liver should be recovered from the waste. Next, lift or roll the animal so any pooled blood in the cavity can drain. Use a clean cloth to wipe the inside of the body. Trim away damaged areas and, if you have access to water, it's a good idea to clean the inside of the carcass. If you do use water to wash the body cavity, always dry off the meat completely. Bacteria grow best in moisture and spoilage can result unless you take precautions.

Skinning

For the best-tasting meat, the carcass should be skinned as soon as possible. If skinned while the body is still warm, the

Photo by Mike Strandlund

In warm weather, it's important to recover your animal and cool the carcass quickly to avoid spoilage.

149

hide will peel off much easier and the meat will cool much faster.

To skin a big game animal, remove the cape first if you wish to preserve the trophy. Caping is done by cutting around the animal's body just behind the front legs, then making an incision from that cut along the backbone to a point just behind the antlers. There, the cut forms a Y extending to each antler. Cuts are made around the top of each leg, and the skin is peeled off with no further cuts in the hide. Carefully remove the skin from the skull, taking special care around the ears, eyes, nostrils, and lips, then salt or freeze immediately. If possible, allow a guide, outfitter or someone with skinning and caping experience to handle your trophy in the field. Unless you have experience or the knowledge to cape an animal's skull, you may wish to leave this chore to your taxidermist; however, prompt attention is necessary in warm weather.

Capes and hides that are to be preserved must be thoroughly salted to prevent hair slippage. Common table salt works well to draw moisture from the hide. Be sure the water drawn out by the salt is allowed to drain from the hide. Hides may be frozen instead of salted but the two preservation methods should never be combined.

If you don't wish to save the cape, you may suspend the animal from either the head or the back legs and take the hide off in one piece. Cuts are made around each lower leg, those cuts are connected by four more cuts to the main belly incision, and the hide can be peeled off.

If you wish to delay skinning until you get home, prop the chest cavity open with a stick. You may wrap the carcass with cloth—cheesecloth, preferably—to keep insects off. Hang the carcass in a cool, shady area where air can circulate and hasten drying and cooling of the meat.

Some hunters prefer to transport their animals to camp or to their homes before field dressing. They say this prevents dirt and dust—along with leaves and twigs—from getting inside the carcass as it's dragged to the closest roadway and hauled by vehicle to the meat pole. If the weather is cool—in the mid 40s—and the drive a short one—less than an hour—this may have some merit. However, in warm or hot weather, the animal should be field-dressed immediately upon recovery. That "wild taste" some people complain about is often the end result of shoddy meat care.

Getting your trophy back to camp or home generally requires muscle power, first involving carrying or dragging dead weight across uneven, sometimes rugged terrain. A hunting buddy can make the task easier and in some instances a pack animal or off-road vehicle may be used. Regardless, it's seldom easy.

In the case of larger animals such as moose or elk, it's likely the animal will be skinned where it fell, then quartered or boned prior to packing the animal out. But most big game animals are simply dragged or carried to the closest roadway.

Dragging an animal can damage the hide or cape unless care is taken. Some hunters prefer to tie the legs of a field-dressed trophy together and use a pole or stout sapling to lift and carry the carcass. One person may be able to carry smaller game animals slung over their shoulders; however, this can be difficult and even dangerous. It's a good idea to tie brightly colored surveyor's tape or a small bell to the carcass or pack to avoid being mistaken for live game by other hunters. But most big game is simply too large for one person to haul any distance without help.

A travois rigged out of cut saplings can make the initial transporting job easier. If the animal is simply dragged from the field or woods, it should be pulled head first. Heavy plastic or a tarp may be placed under the carcass to prevent damage to the hide and to make it slide easier. If ropes are used to tie the head or legs in position, they may rub and ruin the hide unless care is taken.

When transporting the animal by vehicle, do not tie it to the fender, roof, or across the hood. Engine heat and road dust will cause excessive spoilage. Place the carcass in the bed of a pickup or automobile trunk,

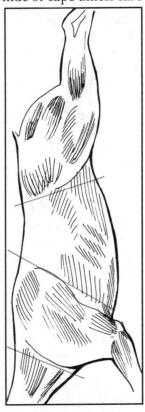

When quartering big game, make the cuts shown above in sequential order. The legs and head are removed first, followed by splitting the backbone and dividing each side into thirds.

leaving the lid partly open for air circulation. Also, always check the local laws before transporting game; some require a part of the carcass be visible. If you have a long distance to drive, allow the carcass to cool thoroughly first.

Keep in mind that the sight of animal carcasses may offend some people. Keep them out of view unless required by law. Treat all big game trophies with the respect they deserve and do your part to improve the image of hunters in the public eye.

Butchering

While many hunters have their big game meat processed by a butcher, others do the job themselves. Most hunters who do it themselves simply debone the meat, separating it into serving-size packages of steaks, roasts, stew meat, and ground meat.

Some hunters recommend aging game animals to improve the quality of the meat. Proper aging requires hanging for a week to 10 days at a temperature of 40 to 45 degrees. Younger animals require less time while older game needs more.

Remember, prompt and proper field care of game animals can provide not only excellent meals but lifelong memories, thanks to the art of taxidermy. You owe it to yourself and the game you hunt to be prepared for the work necessary once the shot is made and the animal is down.

Trophy Recognition

To some, one of the finest accomplishments in bowhunting is to "make the book," or take a big game trophy exceptional enough to be included in the records of the Pope and Young Club, a national organization of bowhunters.

To qualify, antlers and skulls must be "scored" by an official club measurer after a 60 day drying period. If it meets minimum dimensions and other standards, the trophy will be accepted by the club and entered in the recordbook. For more information on the club and its program, write Pope and Young Club, PO Box 548, Chatfield, MN 55923.

The NRA Hunter Recognition Program, operated by NRA Hunter Services Division, awards plaques to bowhunters for taking trophy animals that meet minimum requirements. For entry forms and more information write to the NRA Hunter Recognition Program, National Rifle Association of America, 1600 Rhode Island Avenue NW, Washington, DC 20036-3268, or call 202-828-6240.

CHAPTER 8

BOWHUNTING SMALL GAME, VARMINTS, AND FISH

Photo by Mike Strandlund

Bowhunting for small game and varmints can be even more challenging than big game hunting. They present small targets and are wary and quick-moving.

S mall game, varmints and fish provide excellent off-season sport and can help serious-minded bowhunters become better at scouting, locating, stalking, calling, and shooting game. This type of hunting is an ideal tune-up for big game seasons and many of these animals will provide excellent table fare. Most are challenging to hunt and are memorable trophies in their own right. By expanding your bowhunting horizons beyond that offered by big game, you can find year-round excitement near home and all across this game-rich continent.

Serious bowhunters often hone stalking/shooting skills by seeking out small game targets such as rabbits and squirrels or varmints like groundhogs, ground squirrels, and prairie dogs. Bowhunting for turkeys is one of the fastest-growing phases of the sport. A few bowhunters call coyotes, bobcats, foxes, raccoons, and other predators. Still others take on the ultimate bowhunting marksmanship challenge, hunting for winged targets like pheasant, grouse, quail, and waterfowl.

Small Game Hunting

Rabbits and Squirrels

Rabbits and squirrels are the most popular game in America, but are generally neglected by bowhunters. They are often

Maslowski Photos

Squirrels and rabbits are favorites among small game hunters. Taking them with a bow requires considerable hunting skill and marksmanship.

overlooked in the quest for big game, and are elusive and hard-to-hit targets for archers. But they can provide a lot of challenging, enjoyable hunting in times and places where deer hunting is not available.

A bowhunter gearing up for these small mammals needs a different approach than with big game. The main consideration is bows and arrows. While bows may be of very light weight, it's generally advisable for deer hunters to hunt small game with the same bow they plan to use for deer. The extra practice in the field may pay off from the tree stand.

Arrows may be tipped with broadheads, but the best points for rabbits and squirrels is a blunt or Judo point. These tips impact enough killing shock to an animal to do the job without ruining meat, and prevent arrow losses by keeping shafts from snaking under grass and ground litter. Never use pointed target or field tips for any kind of hunting; they lack both cutting ability and impact energy for a quick kill.

Rabbit and hare hunting is most popular among bowhunters in the winter, after big game seasons have closed. As the thick foliage this game inhabits shrinks, they become easier to find. Spend most of your time looking in clearcuts, briar patches, and thick edge zones. Accumulations of the distinctive tracks and droppings will tell you when you're in good rabbit country.

Bowhunting for rabbits and hares can be done with or without dogs. While traditional cottontail hunting involves beagles, and is very effective for shotgunners, it is much less effective for bowhunters. Beagles tend to keep rabbits on the move, which makes an accurate bow shot very difficult. A good method is to use a larger dog that will flush rabbits but be unable to trail them through the thick cover they inhabit. In such cases, the rabbit will usually run a short distance and stop, giving the archer a chance to sneak into bow range.

Photo by Richard P. Smith

Hares, including snowshoes and jackrabbits, are plentiful in many areas and seasons are long with generous bag limits. That adds up to a lot of bowhunting fun.

155

Most bowhunters prefer to hunt rabbits without dogs, still-hunting through cover, trying to spot game. Look for cotton-tails and jackrabbits in small, thick clumps of cover. When hunting snowshoe hare in winter, concentrate on searching for the small, shiny black eye against the white fur and snow background. The best action is at dawn and dusk, when rabbits emerge from dens and forms to feed.

Squirrel hunting is practiced most by bowhunters as an aside to deer hunting. A bowhunter headed out for a day in the deer woods tucks a couple of "old" arrows, tipped with blunts or Judos, into his quiver on the chance a squirrel presents a shot. Those who hunt exclusively for squirrels take a stand in an oak grove inhabited by bushytails, or maybe on the edge of a cornfield where big fox squirrels feed. Walking through the woods may produce a few shooting opportunities, but not nearly as many as stand hunting. After 15 or 20 minutes standing quietly in camouflage against a big oak trunk, with cooperative weather, squirrels will come out of the "woodwork." Wait for the hyperactive tree dwellers to pause in pursuit of an acorn in the leaves. Shots at squirrels in the treetops produce more lost or broken arrows than makings for squirrel stew.

Treestand hunting for squirrels is quite effective and greatly reduces arrow loss. Squirrels have certain travel routes to and from feeding areas just like deer. Scout these out, erect a stand, and bring plenty of arrows.

Wild Turkeys

Wild turkey populations have grown dramatically across the country in the last couple decades, and so has the popularity of bowhunting them. The attractions of turkey hunting are many: the chance to hunt in spring, the unique method of hunting, the prospects of a turkey dinner. But perhaps the biggest draw to turkey hunting is the challenge. Many experienced, expert bowhunters rank taking a keen-sensed, quick-witted, and always wary and elusive turkey as the toughest challenge and biggest accomplishment in bowhunting.

In autumn, most turkeys that fall to an arrow are taken incidentally by bowhunters after deer. In spring, it's another story. The goal is the wild turkey gobbler. Hunters try to play the tom turkey's spring breeding behavior against him, using calls and decoys that promise satisfaction for his mating urges, luring him into bow range.

Bowhunters need special gear for spring turkey hunting. Most favor a compound bow set up to emphasize pinpoint

Photo by Karen Lollo

Many expert bowhunters agree the turkey is the most difficult game animal to take with a bow. They are keen-eyed, quick, and suspicious of calling and blinds.

accuracy and a light holding weight over fast arrow speed. If a turkey has a chance to duck a shaft, he will do it, with arrow speed making little difference. What will make a difference is the ability to draw when a turkey can't see you, and hold until he reappears.

Arrow points should be special broadheads designed for both cutting and shock. There are a couple of special turkey heads on the market that combine sharp blades with "arrow-stopping" features such as dull inserts or split blades. A string tracker may help recover turkeys, especially those that take flight after being struck by an arrow. But it takes skill and preparation to use these correctly, or they may cause a missed shot or ruined opportunity.

Turkey hunters will also need calls and complete camouflage, and perhaps a decoy, blind, stool, and other accessories. Check your state's laws to be sure decoys and blinds are legal before using them.

The common tactic for spring turkey hunting is to locate a tom by the sound of his gobbling, then sneak in as close as you dare, set up so you can get a shot off unseen, and begin calling. The key is the ability to draw and release on a close-range, called-in bird without being detected. To accomplish this, you may place a decoy near some large tree trunks within good bow range. An approaching gobbler will head for the decoy when he sees it, and you can draw when he's behind a tree. A good blind made of camo cloth will be a great aid if it is well camouflaged and set up correctly.

For more details on turkey hunting, see the NRA Hunter Skills Series book, *Wild Turkey Hunting*.

Photos by Mike Strandlund

Most turkeys taken by bow are gobblers called in during the spring breeding season. The most crucial moment is taking the shot, when it's easy to be seen or to miss the turkey's small vital zone. Wait until the bird's head is hidden before moving into shooting position, and aim for the largest vital zone—the wing butt/spinal cord.

Varmint and Predator Hunting

Varmint and predator hunting is valuable to the bowhunter. It provides many hours of enjoyment, is great off-season practice, and in some cases provides monetary rewards in the form of valuable furs.

The variety of ground-dwelling rodents—woodchucks, prairie dogs, and the like—are pests to agriculture and make challenging targets for an archer to stalk and shoot. The larger species are also edible when prepared correctly.

Calling predators—coyotes, fox, bobcats, and coon—is growing in popularity among bowhunters. Predator hunters locate prime habitat for their prey, carefully set up to avoid scent, sight or sound detection, and begin operating a rabbit distress cry or similar call. Complete camo and knowledge of the animal's habits are key to getting the necessary close-range shot.

Maslowski Photo

Marmots, chucks, and ground squirrels provide good hunting action in the off-season. They provide the bowhunter with live-game practice and are surprisingly edible.

Photo by Richard P. Smith   *Photo by Mike Strandlund*

An exciting winter sport is bowhunting predators—coyotes, bobcats, fox, and other carnivores. The animals are usually called into bow range with a mouth blown rabbit distress call or electronic caller.

Expert callers recommend hunting predators at night when possible. If legal, a bowhunter can use a spotlight with red lens (the color is invisible to most game) to locate animals approaching in the dark. Instinctive shooting is best for this type of hunting, because a lighted target and dark surroundings are conducive to sightless shooting.

Wingshooting with Bow and Arrow

An advanced type of bowhunting different from all other approaches is wingshooting. Taking a flying pheasant, dove, quail, duck or partridge with a bow and arrow is a feat that requires well-practiced skill and a certain amount of natural talent.

Yet, a fair number of archers can hit soaring targets with consistency. Most who do rely on instinctive shooting and longbows or recurves. The let-off compound with sights is a handicap where quick snap-shots are called for and mechanical sighting is futile.

To practice for wingshooting, have a friend toss heavy cardboard disks into the air to simulate flying birds. There are mechanical disk throwers available that vault disks in a path simulating the flight of a gamebird.

For both targets and real game, most wingshooters employ flu-flu arrows. The large, often spiralled fletching on flu-flus allows fairly normal arrow flight for 20 or 30 yards, then kills arrow velocity dramatically with air resistance. Arrows drop within sight and are much easier to find. In hunting, some archers use another wingshooting arrow feature, the bird point. The bird point is a blunt tip with large, cloverleaf-shaped wires looping to the sides that break necks and wings of birds and give the archer considerably more room for error.

Favorite flying targets among bowhunters are pheasants and geese. They offer large, close, relatively slow-flying targets when hunted correctly. Pheasants are best hunted with a pointing dog, to locate and pin down the bird, allowing hunters to get positioned and ready to shoot. You can also use a close-working flusher or retriever, or just walk through the cornfields and high-grass sloughs or thickets where pheasants frequent, constantly ready for the whirr of wings and cackle of a flushed rooster.

Geese, primarily Canadas, are generally hunted from blinds in fields filled with dozens or hundreds of decoys. Hunters call to passing flocks, hoping to lure geese into bow range.

The key to success here is waiting for the right shot; under ideal conditions the geese will attempt to land, and taking your shot just before they touch down (or just after, if legal) is your best bet.

Some bowhunters occasionally take ducks, grouse, doves, and other winged targets, but these fast-moving targets are usually too elusive for an archer. Arrows not only have a hard time hitting their mark; they have a hard time even catching up with it!

Bowfishing

Bowfishing has a loyal and growing group of participants, thanks to the long seasons, shooting action, and generous bag limits it offers. Rough fish such as carp, gar, suckers, and buffalo are primary bowfishing targets, but certain saltwater species including sharks and rays are also popular.

Bows used for bowfishing may be any make, model, and weight. Many shooters seem to prefer recurves because the action often calls for quick, rapid-fire, and the simplicity of stick bows is an advantage. Reels mounted to the bow allow heavy, solid glass or metal arrows to be shot through or past the reel. Arrows typically have no fletching at all and attach to the reel by a sturdy line that allows the arrow—and the fish—

Photos by Karl Gunzer Jr.

Bowfishing has increased greatly in popularity in recent years. Bow-fishermen use special equipment—fiberglass arrows, barbed points, line, and reels—to take rough fish and saltwater species that can be found near the surface or lured close.

to be retrieved. Barbed fish heads, made to hold the fish securely on the arrow, come in a variety of designs.

For carp or smaller fish, most types of fish points and cord with a spool is sufficient. Take care that line does not run out or tangle while your arrow is airborne. It may spring back and end up behind you—or worse. If you're going for larger sea quarry such as sharks or rays, you may need a reel, special broadhead-type points, and more heavy duty equipment.

When fish are near the surface, they aren't hard to hit for archers who have tuned and practiced with their bowfishing equipment. But light refraction makes underwater fish appear closer to the surface than they really are. The deeper they are, the more the refraction is pronounced. Archers must remember to shoot well below the image they see if they hope to arrow an underwater fish.

Carp, an import from Europe that has exploded in population and has become a nuisance fish throughout America, is the most popular bowfishing target. Along with their native American cousin the buffalofish, carp prefer calm or slow-moving waters with muddy bottoms. Suckers inhabit faster-moving, colder waters in rocky streams. When these "rough" fish typically spawn in the spring, the shallows come alive with wallowing, finny targets. Waders and boats can help get shooters within bow range, but stalking the banks or just taking up strategic stands will work as well at times.

In the Deep South, the primitive, heavily-armored gar is the prime target of bowfishermen. There are several varieties, ranging from the smallish 2 to 3-foot spotted gar, to the monstrous alligator gar that can outweigh his pursuer. These fish inhabit slow-moving rivers, swamps and bayous, and are often taken as they laze in the sun just below the water's surface. For big gar, a bowfisherman should use very heavy line attached not to his bow's reel, but to a float. If a big fish is arrowed and peels all the line from a reel, it will detach from the bow and pull a float into the water. The bowfisherman can pursue the float and perhaps put another arrow into the fish before trying to boat it.

Floats are also used for the big saltwater species pursued by bowfishermen: sharks, rays, and gamefish that can be found at the surface and can be legally bowhunted. In saltwater bowfishing, the common tactic is to ease slowly through quiet bays, taking shots as prey is taken by surprise. Sharks are also sometimes bowhunted by baiting and chumming.

While many bowfishermen use their harvest mainly for fertilizer or cat food, virtually all fish can be eaten. Carp is wrongly disdained in America as a "trash" fish, but is considered a delicacy in other parts of the world. Large carp or those from warm, polluted waters are usually unsuitable for the table, but others may be delicious when prepared correctly. One method used to judge a rough fish's palatability is to sniff the gills of a freshly taken fish. A fresh smell means the fish will taste fine; a rank or musty odor suggests you feed the fish to a cat or your tomato plants.

Bowfishing tournaments are held in many parts of the country and attract hundreds of shooters. Chambers of commerce have sponsored bowfishing tournaments as a way of attracting business during a slow time of year and to help clean up local waterways of a destructive fish.

CHAPTER 9

BOWHUNTING SAFETY AND ETHICS

If you're the optimistic type who believes accidents only happen to other people, you probably won't get much out of this chapter. But if you're honest enough to admit that people who felt exactly the same way have been hurt—and *killed*—while bowhunting, you may benefit from the following safety rules and common sense advice.

Bowhunters are often their own worst enemies. Many prefer to hunt alone in remote, backcountry areas. They climb hills, mountains, and trees. They hunt in good weather and bad. They carry razor-sharp hunting arrows and skinning knives. They often go without adequate food and sleep. They routinely over-exert themselves and, on occasion, take unnecessary chances. Little wonder mishaps occur.

Get into the habit of using safe bowhunting procedures, such as raising and lowering bow and arrows with a haul line when hunting from a tree stand. Safety should always be the first consideration.

Cuts and falls account for the majority of bowhunting accidents. Others waiting to happen typically involve faulty or damaged equipment, lapses in judgment, the animals being hunted and, finally, other bowhunters. Fortunately, most bowhunting injuries are minor, but some are serious and even fatal. Almost every accident can be traced to a moment of inattention or carelessness. This is why you must take the responsibility for your own safety—and that of others—each time you pick up your bow and head for the door.

Generally, bowhunting is a very safe shooting sport. Awareness of all potential problems and conscientious efforts to avoid these pitfalls can go a long way to making it even safer. Four types of safety must be observed while bowhunting: shooting safety, equipment safety, hunting safety, and safety afield.

Shooting Safety

A standard rule of shooting safety warns you never to draw an arrow and aim at anything you don't intend to shoot. It's a good rule, considering the case of the man who eagerly tore open the cardboard mailing container and withdrew the new compound bow he'd ordered several weeks earlier. Removing its plastic covering, he hefted the bow and smiled admiringly across the room at his wife. He picked up a practice arrow, nocked it and extended his arm—just to get the feel of the new bow. Aiming at a window, he slowly came to full draw–and accidentally released the arrow! The sounds of his wife's scream and breaking glass were the next things he remembered. Although the arrow missed his wife before shattering the window pane on the far side of the living room, it could have been much worse.

Photo by Richard P. Smith

Before learning to shoot or trying new equipment, make sure you're familiar with safe shooting practices and the particular gear you're using.

Always be conscious of the flight path of an arrow. All shooting should be done only in areas where there is no danger to personal property, pets, livestock, or other people. Aim only at targets you want to hit and be certain there is a suitable backstop to halt errant shots. Remember, an arrow is easily deflected and may ricochet wildly beyond the target area. Following are additional shooting safety tips:

- Never shoot an arrow straight up, even in an open field. Modern bows can easily shoot an arrow out of sight and a falling arrow could kill or injure anyone in its path.
- Avoid shots at skylined targets or game. Although an arrow's range may be more limited than a firearm, a missed shot can do deadly damage within its effective range. If you can't see and know for certain what lies beyond your target, pass up the shot.
- Don't draw your bow to shoot if anyone is standing anywhere between you and the target. Never, under any circumstances, aim a drawn bow at another person.
- Be aware of the penetrating power of broadhead-tipped arrows. At close range a hunting arrow has more penetrating power than a bullet. A sandbank is perhaps the best backstop for broadheads, although special broadhead targets are manufactured and available.

Keeping these standard rules of shooting safety in mind, we next turn our attention to equipment. As already noted, many bowhunting injuries are self-inflicted. Faulty equipment is one major cause of injury.

Photo by Richard P. Smith

Use extreme care when handling broadheads. If they're as sharp as they should be, it will be very easy to cut yourself—or worse.

167

Equipment Safety

Modern archery tackle is generally well made and can stand normal in-the-field abuse; however, periodic checking of equipment can eliminate problems before they occur. More than one bowhunter has been hurt when his bow literally exploded in his hands as he brought it to full draw. Cracked arrows have splintered at the moment of release and pierced the shooter's bow hand.

The following are a few do's and don'ts to keep in mind when handling your hunting equipment.

- Don't shoot any bow with frayed bowstrings or cut strands. Weakened bowstrings can suddenly break, damaging the bow and injuring the shooter. Replace any strings showing signs of wear, especially around the loops or serving. Cables on all compound bows deserve close attention, too. Replace worn or damaged cables immediately.

- Routinely check bow limbs and riser sections. Small cracks or separations indicate weakness in the wood or fiberglass. Other signs of possible trouble are flaking or chipping. At times the laminations will separate. Never draw a bow showing evidence of weakness.

- Discard any cracked or severely bent arrow. A weakened arrow is dangerous to shoot as it may break and penetrate the shooter's bow hand at the instant of release as the shaft comes under tremendous force.

- Always use a bow stringer to string and unstring a recurve or longbow. The step-through stringing method can twist the bow's limbs, damaging them. The push-pull stringing method is dangerous if a string loop or a hand slips. Severe facial injuries–even blindness–can result if the limb snaps back and strikes the face of the person attempting to string the bow.

- Never—under any circumstances—draw and release any bow without an arrow on the string. This is called "dry firing" and may result in serious damage to the bow. Also, be sure to check arrow nocks for cracks before and after practice shots. A weakened plastic nock can break at the instant of release and result in dry firing.

- Don't forget to check and tighten the bolts and screws on compound bows. Examine axles, idler wheels, and cams for signs of wear or damage. Lubricate moving parts as required. Use bowstring wax often to prolong string life.

Check the arrow for cracks and bends if you think it may have hit something hard. A damaged arrow can come apart as you release it, sending pieces into your hand or arm.

- Store your equipment properly. Never stand any bow in a corner or place it on its limb tip for extended periods of time. Hang bows horizontally on bow racks or suspend them vertically from hooks or nails. Store arrows in arrow boxes if possible, or upright in special arrow racks. Unstring longbows and recurves if they won't be used soon; check adjustable-weight compound bow instructions for extended storage advice. Some manufacturers suggest lowering the draw weight of these bows before storage.

Proper care of bowhunting equipment can prolong its life and help prevent needless injuries. Of course, you and other bowhunters must assume responsibility for your own safety in the field.

Hunting Safety

Since most bowhunting injuries are self-inflicted, savvy men and women take common sense steps to avoid accidents. But they also realize they are sharing the field with other people who may not be so careful or conscientious. They practice what may be called "defensive bowhunting." Seriously consider these preventive measures.

Carry a small light when walking to or from your stand in darkness. Otherwise a hunter or poacher may mistake you for game. Unfortunately, a few accidental shootings—and several deaths—have resulted when excited hunters have released arrows at shadowy shapes moving past their stands. Special clip-on or pin-on safety lights can be worn on hunting clothes to prevent tragic mistakes. A small light is not likely to frighten game. Some hunters place red or amber filters over the flashlight lens, since game animals cannot distinguish such colored light. Either way, carrying a light is good insurance against accidents.

While crossing rough or unfamiliar terrain, your light serves a dual purpose by detecting barriers, obstacles, and unseen hazards. Each year a few stubborn bowhunters are injured when they refuse to use a light and suffer the consequences.

Photo by F. R. Martin

If you're hunting with a buddy in the same general area, be sure to keep tabs on their whereabouts. Never release an arrow at game standing in the direction of your partner's position. An overshot or a deflection could mean disaster. No animal is worth it.

Besides these defensive tactics, you should remember the following rules of safe bow handling and bowhunting:

- Never walk with an arrow nocked unless you are actually stalking game. Every year bowhunters injure themselves–and others—by falling on nocked arrows

While hiking, keep all your arrows in your quiver. With broadheads exposed, you risk slipping and impaling yourself.

or thoughtlessly mishandling broadheadtipped arrows with people standing nearby. Walking with an arrow on the bowstring is especially dangerous in wet or snowy weather and while crossing rough or uneven terrain.

- Avoid bow quivers that don't provide protective covering for your broadheads. Never wear a back, hip, or belt quiver if riding horseback or in an open motorized vehicle. A fall onto your arrows could be fatal.

- Use a broadhead wrench to remove, mount or handle broadheads. To do their job effectively, broadheads must be razor-sharp. Always treat them with the respect they deserve.

- Take care in field-dressing arrow-killed game. Account for sharp broadheads and blades before reaching into the animal's body cavity. Be careful with your knife as well, especially when applying pressure necessary to cut through tendons and cartilage. Always cut away from yourself.

- Take special caution when calling game. Calls may attract hunters as well as animals and a concealed caller may be stalked and accidentally shot.

Photo by Mike Strandlund

When field-dressing game, be careful your knife doesn't slip, and watch out for broadheads or pieces of arrow shaft that may be broken off inside the body cavity.

- Dress appropriately if you are sharing the field with hunters using firearms. A completely camouflaged bowhunter may be inviting trouble. It's smart to wear a bit of fluorescent orange clothing or other highly visible color and in some areas game laws mandate appropriate attire.
- Don't climb a gate or fence while carrying your bow. Treat it as you would a loaded firearm, sliding it under or through the fence and laying it where you can't possibly fall on it. If hunting with a buddy, take turns holding the bows and climbing.

Tree Stand Safety

Since hunting from trees and elevated stands has become so popular, bowhunters do a considerable amount of climbing. Each year some meet death or paralysis when they fall. Tree stand safety is important enough to warrant special attention here.

Photos by Mike Strandlund

Portable tree stands must be set up and operated correctly to avoid the inherent dangers in using them.

Some bowhunters are ill-prepared for climbing in and out of trees. Others simply disregard commonsense rules of tree stand hunting safety. A few have had their lives ended—or changed forever—by a fall. Here are some ways you can prevent tragedy when hunting from trees.

- Never attempt to climb while carrying your bow. Keep both hands completely free; place your bow and any other equipment away from the tree's base. A fall while climbing is bad enough. Landing on your own gear is doubly dangerous.
- Use a strong cord or line to raise and lower equipment from your stand. You can tie one end to your belt during your climb.
- Always wear a safety line or belt around your waist when in any elevated stand. Fasten it before you climb into your stand and wear it until you're ready to climb down.
- Be especially careful climbing and descending. Realize that tree limbs can snap under your weight, even if they've held in the past. Use sturdy portable tree steps, if possible. Use extra caution in frigid or wet weather when steps may be slippery and fingers numbed from the cold.
- Never hunt from trees during thunderstorms.
- Don't be tempted to climb into any permanent stand you find. Such stands weaken with age and may collapse under your weight.
- Place portable stands securely and properly in position. Follow all stand assembly and installation directions. Tighten all nuts before the season begins and after the stand is removed at season's end.

Photo by Joe Workosky

- If you use climbing steps, always place the last step parallel or slightly above the level of the stand. This way you will not have to step up into the stand, or down from the stand, which is especially difficult in fading light.
- Be sure there is adequate clearance to draw and shoot your bow. A bow may be damaged—or the shooter knocked off balance—if a bow limb hits a branch at the instant of release.

A safety harness should be standard equipment for the tree stand hunter. Falls from trees are one of the leading causes of accidents among bowhunters.

- Should you accidentally drop an arrow while on stand, don't forget about it when climbing down. It could fall point-up and result in a nasty cut—or worse—should you happen to jump or step down on the shaft as you leave your stand.

Safety Afield

It's always a good idea to let somebody know where you'll be hunting and when you expect to return. In an emergency, valuable time can be saved in locating you. This is mandatory in remote areas, but it's a smart routine to follow even when hunting close to home. Other safety concerns arise any time one deals with the elements of nature.

Hypothermia

Hypothermia, or severe loss of body heat, is the number one killer of outdoorsmen. Consider the lightly dressed bowhunter who travelled to the state forest a few hours from home to hunt one warm afternoon in October. After following heavily used deer trails into a thicket, he selected a stand location. Surprised by a six pointer shortly before dark, his shot was slightly off the mark. As the cool drizzle started, he quickly followed the blood trail so it would not wash away. Hours later, cold from rain, exhausted from searching, and lost, the hunter sat shivering in the dropping temperatures. Without flashlight or emergency gear, the hunter lapsed into unconsciousness. Next morning he was dead.

Hypothermia can occur any time the temperature is below 60 degrees, and is influenced by moisture, wind, and fatigue. Persons suffering from hypothermia go through stages beginning with shivering and progressing to loss of muscular control, mental confusion, and unconsciousness. Victims may turn blue and be unable to speak.

Photo by Richard P. Smith

Cold or wet weather requires special considerations to avoid hypothermia. Always be prepared for the worst.

If you or any of your hunting companions exhibit any of these signs, treatment must be administered immediately. Get the victim out of the weather and into shelter. Remove any wet clothing and replace with dry clothes. Protect the head and neck from any further heat loss. If the victim shows only mild symptoms get him near a heat source, or put him in a warm sleeping bag. If the victim is semiconscious or unconscious, place him naked in a sleeping bag, remove your clothes, get into the bag, and lie against the person. Always seek prompt, professional medical attention for victims with symptoms of advanced hypothermia. Never give alcohol to a victim of hypothermia.

To help avoid hypothermia, wear clothes that offer good protection against the elements, dress in layers, and avoid getting wet. Don't overexert yourself, as fatigue contributes to hypothermia. Always carry matches or a lighter in case of emergency.

Special Considerations

More and more smart hunters also carry a daypack or fanny pack containing emergency items. Even experienced hunters have become lost or injured and forced to rely on their own resources for survival. Such packs commonly contain signaling devices such as a whistle or mirror; security devices such as a space blanket and waterproofed matches; snack items like a

Photo by Richard P. Smith

If you're planning to hunt around water, there is a whole new set of safety rules you must observe.

175

chocolate or granola bar; and extra clothing such as a rain poncho, shirt or sweater and a change of socks. Most veteran woodsmen routinely carry a compass and often have topo maps in their pack.

Archery seasons open early in many areas, leading to thousands of encounters with poisonous snakes. If you are in an area frequented by snakes, be sure to know proper snake bite care. If you're far away from medical attention, carry a snake bite kit or venom extractor.

People who become lost often panic, compounding the problem by aimless or desperate wandering. The best general advice is to stay put and, conditions permitting, build a fire—smoky by day and bright by night. If a spouse, hunting buddy, or landowner knows your schedule and area, help will be forthcoming if you fail to return as planned.

Finally, unusual exertion–or even the pulse-pounding excitement of the hunt—can put a strain on any hunter's heart. People in poor to average physical condition as well as those under a doctor's care should recognize the need to take it easy. It's plain foolish to try to climb a ridge in record time, drag out a heavy animal, or prove you're Superhunter in any similar manner.

Again, bowhunting is a relatively safe sport, so try your best to keep it that way by following these standard rules of safety and by fully preparing yourself before you pick up your bow and head out the door.

Hunting Ethics

Ethics become increasingly important as hunters come under the close scrutiny of anti-hunting groups and the general public. Hunters are responsible not only to themselves, but to other hunters, landowners, the general public, and the game

Photo by Richard P. Smith

Game animals deserve the greatest amount of respect from a hunter. If there isn't a bit of remorse mixed in with the exhilaration of making the kill, you're missing the essence of hunting.

they hunt. While certain basic ethical standards are incorporated into hunting laws and regulations, every hunter must also have his or her own personal set of ethics within these laws.

Many ethical questions have obvious answers, even if they're not covered by regulations. Others aren't so easy. To help set your own standards, ask, is it legal, or is it fair to everyone concerned, including the game, other people, and myself?

Responsibilities to Other Hunters

Besides safety, you have several other responsibilities to fellow bowhunters. If you find another hunter where you planned to hunt, find another stand. It's counter-productive to challenge him to the spot. Hopefully, another hunter will someday show you the same respect.

Try to pass on responsible hunting behavior to fellow hunters. If you witness one of your companions being disrespectful, correct him tactfully. If he fails to change his behavior, refuse to hunt with him.

Don't litter, drive vehicles where others may be hunting, or otherwise disturb others. Most hunters have deep feelings for nature and the peace of mind they find while hunting. Don't violate them.

Responsibilities to Landowners

Every year, thousands of acres of private land are posted off-limits because hunters treated the land or its owner with disrespect. This hurts all hunters as it becomes more and more difficult to find land to hunt.

Always get permission before hunting on any private property. Approach the landowner with respect; don't show up in hunting attire at 6:30 a.m. on the opening morning of bow season. Ask for permission to hunt several months before the season and you'll have a better chance of obtaining permission. Once you get permission, treat the land with utmost respect. Leave no signs you were there—pick up any litter you find, even if its not yours. Don't construct unsightly tree stands or cut trees without permission. Don't drive on soft ground and leave tire ruts.

Other ways to keep good landowner relations are to avoid disturbing livestock, fences, crops, and other property. Don't abuse your welcome by bringing a carload of companions or hunting on the land day after day. A token of appreciation such as a gift, a card, or offer to help with chores goes a long

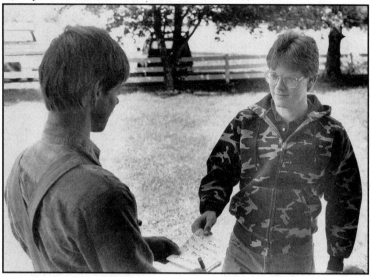

Always seek permission before hunting on private property.

way toward being welcome next year, and will promote a positive image for the hunter.

Responsibilities to the Public

Remember that the environment and animals belong to everyone, not just hunters. Respect the rights of people who enjoy nature without hunting—avoid shooting in areas where you know nonhunters are enjoying the outdoors. Keep gut piles and other signs of hunting out of view. Don't display bagged animals to people who may not want to see them. Remember that unfavorable public opinion has resulted in laws and regulations that have hurt hunters.

Another duty the hunter owes the public is to ensure the enforcement of game laws. Hunters must abide by the laws and report those who trespass, poach animals, shoot road signs, or otherwise vandalize property.

The most important duty a hunter owes the public is safety. An arrow is as deadly as any rifle bullet, be sure of your target-and what is beyond—before you shoot. Avoid shots which may deflect in a dangerous direction.

Responsibilities to the Game

The game animal is more than a resource to be harvested; it is a magnificent wild animal deserving utmost respect. Hunters

178

who do not feel a deep reverence for wildlife and an obligation to conserve the resource are missing the essence of hunting.

Never take a shot that has a better chance of crippling than killing. Always wait for your best shot, and don't shoot beyond your effective bow range. Don't shoot an animal if another is standing directly behind it. Broadhead tipped arrows have tremendous penetrating power and could pass through the first animal and wound or kill the second. Always look for antlers before shooting in a bucks- or bulls- only zone.

If you hit an animal and can't find it, exhaust all possible efforts for recovery. Don't be afraid to ask an experienced bowhunter for assistance. Most will be more than glad to help. Help in the conservation and propagation of game. You'll conserve and promote hunting in the process.

Responsibilities to Yourself

Never forget your responsibilities to yourself. If a certain law or hunting regulation conflicts with your well-considered ethical beliefs, work to change that law. Fight it with letters and votes, not disobedience.

Photo by Richard P. Smith

You owe it to the game to wait for the right shot. Taking shots when the animal is too far away or in a poor position risks wounding, rather than killing, the animal.

179

Hunting license fees and taxes on sporting goods are the chief sources of funds for conservation programs, such as providing winter range and feed for elk. In other words, hunters pay for conservation, and are responsible for today's healthy populations of wildlife.

Don't compromise or violate you ethics in a way you may regret later. Hunt hard, honestly, and be proud of your sportsmanship.

Pass Along the Tradition

If you're a hunter in the truest sense, you will eventually reach a point where you derive the most hunting satisfaction from introducing others to the sport. It may be acquainting a friend with hunting, taking a young boy or girl on their first hunt, or volunteering in a hunter education program.

Talk with the new hunter about hunting responsibilities and ethics that all hunters should abide. Show respect for game by never taking a chancy shot, by making every effort to recover a wounded animal, and by never wasting bagged game. Make him or her realize why they must also treat landowners and the general public with respect, to prevent prejudice against hunters. Instruct new hunters early on safety, ethics and responsibility because their respect and appreciation of our hunting heritage will determine the future of hunting.

Photo by Karl Gunzer Jr.

Photo by Richard P. Smith

Young people hold the future of our hunting heritage—teach them to hunt hard, honestly, and respect wildlife.

Appendix

THE NRA AND HUNTING

The National Rifle Association of America encourages and supports sport hunting through a wide variety of programs and services.

The NRA Hunter Services Division assists state and provincial hunter education programs with support materials and training programs for professional and volunteer staff. NRA Hunter Clinics answer the demand for advanced education by emphasizing skills, responsibility, and safety as applied to hunting techniques and game species. The Hunter Information Service communicates to the members a variety of information necessary to plan and complete hunts. The NRA Youth Hunter Education Challenge offers a series of events on the local, state, and national levels to challenge young hunters, through hunting simulated events, to apply basic skills learned in the classroom. The NRA Hunter Recognition Program offers awards to hunters for all levels of hunting achievement. Financial support for wildlife management and shooting sports research is available through the NRA Grants-in-Aid Program.

The NRA Institute for Legislative Action protects the legal rights of hunters. NRA Publications provides a variety of printed material on firearms, equipment and techniques for hunters, including American Hunter magazine, the largest periodical in the U.S. devoted to hunting. Junior programs encourage young people to participate in hunting. Special insurance benefits are available to NRA hunting members, and hunters can further benefit by joining an NRA hunting club or by affiliating an existing club with the NRA. The NRA works with other hunting organizations to sustain a positive image of hunting as a traditional form of recreation, to combat anti-hunting efforts, and to promote a life-long interest in hunting.

For further information, contact the National Rifle Association of America, Hunter Services Division, 1600 Rhode Island Avenue, N.W., Washington, D.C. 20036-3268. Telephone (202) 828-6240.

NRA MATERIALS FOR THE BOWHUNTER

The following are materials available from the NRA Sales Department and can help you prepare your next bowhunting trip.

DESCRIPTION	ITEM NO.	UNIT PRICE
The Hunter's Guide	HE5N5090	$8.95 each
NRA Hunter Skills Series		
Student Manual		
Bowhunting	HS5N5403	$5.00 each
Muzzleloader Hunting	HS5N5145	$5.00 each
Whitetail Deer Hunting	HS5N5047	$5.00 each
Western Big Game Hunting	HS5N5207	$5.00 each
Waterfowl Hunting	HS5N5083	$5.00 each
Wild Turkey Hunting	HS5N5707	$5.00 each
Hardbound Version		
Bowhunting	HS5N5449	$14.95 each
Muzzleloader Hunting	HS5N5172	$14.95 each
Wild Turkey Hunting	HS5N5734	$14.95 each
NRA Hunter Clinic Video		
Collection (VHS)		
Brochure/Order Form	HS3N8108	N/C
Formula For Success: Bowhunting	HS5N7152	$19.95
Bowhunting For Trophy Whitetails	HS5N7205	$19.95
Bowhunting For Whitetail Deer	HS5N7081	$19.95
Life Size Game Targets*		
Brochure/Order Form	HS3N0017	N/C
Package containing one each:		
Whitetail Deer, Turkey, Duck,		
Rabbit, Groundhog, Mule Deer		
Black Bear, Pronghorn,		
Javelina, Coyote, Red Fox,		
Pheasant,and Squirrel	HS5N1283	$7.00

*Note: Various package quantities are available.

DESCRIPTION	ITEM NO.	UNIT PRICE
Other Brochures		
NRA Hunter Recognition Awards	HI3N0106	N/C
Wild Game From Field to Table	HI3N0080	N/C
The Hunter and Wildlife	HI3N0071	N/C
Landowner Relations	HE3N0033	N/C
Responsible Hunting	HE3N0024	N/C
Hypothermia	HE3N0079	N/C
Fitness and Nutrition	HE3N0097	N/C
Water Safety	HE3N0051	N/C
Tree Stand Safety	HE3N0015	N/C
Hunting's Future? It's Up to You	HE3N0159	N/C
NRA and Hunting	HI3N0115	N/C
NRA Hunter Services Division		
Materials Price List	HI3N8091	N/C
NRA Standard Order Form	XS7N8000	N/C

ORDERING INFORMATION

- Use the NRA Standard Order Form to order items listed. Prices are subject to change without notice.

- Prices do not include shipping and handling charges. Certain state sales taxes are applicable.

- Order forms and current prices are available from NRA Sales Department, P.O. Box 5000, Kearneysville, WV 25430-5000 or call **toll free 1-800-336-7402.** VA residents call **toll free 1-800 535-9982.** Hours: 9:00 a.m. to 5:00 p.m. Eastern time.

FUTURE NRA MATERIALS
FOR THE
BOWHUNTER

Other items for the bowhunter soon to be available from the NRA Sales Department:

NRA Hunter Skills Series

NRA Bowhunter Clinic Instructor's Manual
NRA Hunter Clinic Camouflage Cap (Summer) and T-Shirt

THE NRA HUNTER SKILLS SERIES

The NRA Hunter Skills Series is a developing library of books on hunting, shooting, and related activities. It supports the NRA Hunter Clinic Program, a national network of seminars conducted by the NRA Hunter Services Division and volunteer hunter clinic instructors.

The hunter training manuals are developed by NRA staff, with the assistance of noted hunting experts, hunter educators, experienced outdoor writers, and representatives of hunting/conservation organizations. The publications are available in student (bound) and instructor (loose leaf) editions.

The program is planned to include clinics and support material on hunting whitetail deer, waterfowl, wild turkey, small game, predators, upland game, western big game, and others. It will also address marksmanship and hunting with rifle, shotgun, muzzleloader, handgun, and archery equipment.

For more information about the NRA Hunter Clinic Program and its training materials, contact the National Rifle Association of America, Hunter Services Division, 1600 Rhode Island Avenue, N.W., Washington D.C. 20036-3268. Telephone(202) 828-6240.

NRA Big Game Hunter Awards

Let the NRA Big Game Hunter Awards Program help preserve the excitement and memories of some of your best hunts. This program emphasizes the hunter's skills and quality of the hunt–not trophy size. Minimum requirements for all 14 categories of North American big game that are accepted for these awards are listed below. The program recognizes achievement in four different hunting methods:

Bow and Arrow
Modern Firearm—Long Gun
Modern Firearm—Handgun
Muzzleloading Firearm

Beautifully designed certificates mounted on walnut plaques are personalized with the hunt method, hunter's name, animal category and the year and the state or province of the hunt.

REQUIREMENTS

CATEGORY	INDEX FOR DETERMINING STATUS	REQUIREMENTS
Black Bear	Greatest width plus	16 inches
Cougar	length of skull	12 inches
Grizzly and Brown Bear	without jaw	18 inches
Elk	Minimum numbers	5
Mule Deer	of points	4
Black-tailed Deer	on at least	3
Whitetailed Deer	one side	4
Coues Whitetailed Deer	of rack	3
Moose	Greatest spread	40 inches
Caribou	Maximum inside spread	30 inches
Pronghorn	Length of	11 inches
Rocky Mountain Goat	longest horn	8 inches
Native Wild Sheep	Extent of curl	¾
Wild Turkey	Beard length	8 inches

For more information on the NRA Big Game Hunter Awards refer to the NRA Hunter Recognition Program brochure (HI3N0106) or contact the National Rifle Association of America, Hunter Services Division, 1600 Rhode Island Avenue, N.W., Washington D.C. 20036-3268. Telephone (202) 828-6240.

A Guide To
BOWHUNTING ACROSS NORTH AMERICA

The following chart gives general dates for special big game hunting seasons with the bow only. Be sure to check with the state or provincial wildlife agency for specific season dates before you plan your hunt. Many agencies set seasons by management unit or zone, and these may change from one year to the next. Most states and Canadian provinces also allow bowhunting during the regular firearms season.

STATE/PROVINCE SPECIAL BOWHUNTING SEASONS	BOWHUNTING RESTRICTIONS

United States

Alabama
Deer-(mid Oct-late Jan)

75% let-off at full draw maximum; 35 lb. draw weight minimum; 7/8 in. width & 100 gr. weight broadhead (barbless) minimum; 24 in. arrow length minimum

Alaska
No special seasons; See regs for special archery areas

Bow must cast broadhead tipped arrow 175 yd. horizontally minimum; 7/8 in. width broadhead minimum

Arizona
Deer-(end Aug-mid Sep & mid Dec-end Jan)
Pronghorn-(end Aug-early Sep)
Elk-(mid-late Sep & mid-late Nov)
Turkey-(late Aug-mid Sep & late Apr-mid May)
Javelina-(1 week late Feb) Select units (all Jan)

40 lb. pound draw weight minimum;7/8 in. width broadhead minimum

Arkansas
Deer-State wide(early Oct-end Feb)
Some zones (early Oct-end Dec)
Black Bear-(mid-end Oct)
Wild Turkey-(begin Oct-end Feb)

40 lb. draw weight minimum; 7/8 in. width broadhead minimum

California
Deer-Central Coast (early-late Jul)
South Coast (early-late Sep)
Other Areas (mid Aug-mid Sep)
Antelope-(mid-late Aug)
Elk-By permits only (Aug-Dec)

Bows must cast arrow (except flu-flu) 130 yd. minimum; 7/8 in. width broadhead minimum

Colorado
Deer & Elk-(late Aug-late Sep)
Plains Deer-(early-mid Oct & early-late Nov)
Antelope-(mid Aug-late Sep)
Bighorn Sheep-(mid Aug-early Oct)
Mountain Goat-(early Sep-early Oct)

7/8 in. width broadhead (2 cutting edges on same plane) minimum

Connecticut
    Deer & Turkey-(early Oct-
            mid Nov & Dec)

Bow must cast arrow (400 gr.
weight) 150 yd. minimum; 7/8
in. width broadhead (2 blades)
minimum

Delaware
    Deer-(early Sep-mid Oct &
        mid Oct-early Nov)

7/8 in. width broadhead minimum

Florida
    Deer-Northwest Zone (mid Nov)
    Deer-Central Zone (late Sep-
        late Oct)
        South Zone (early Sep-
        early Oct)
    Bear-Limited (mid Nov-late Jan)
    Wild Hog-(dates vary)
    See regs

No explosive or poison
components; no dogs while
bowhunting; no possession of
bow & arrow on airboat in
Dade County during bow season

Georgia
    Deer-(mid Sep-mid Oct)
    Bear-(late Sep-early Dec)

40 lb. draw weight at 28 in. draw
length minimum; 7/8 in. width
broadhead minimum

Hawaii
    Mouflon Sheep-Hawaii(Jul)
    Axis Deer-Lanai (2nd & 3rd
        Sun-Feb)
    Feral Pig-Kauai (Sep & Feb)
        Maui & Hawaii
        (year round)
    Feral Goat-Kauai & Hawaiii
        (year round)
    Feral Sheep-Hawaii
        (year round)
    Mouflon Sheep-Lanai (1st &
        2nd Sun-Aug)

Straight bow 45 lb. draw weight,
compound 30 lb. draw weight &
laminated/full recurve 35 lb.
draw weight minimums; no
explosives or poisoned heads;
broadheads only

Idaho
    Deer & Elk-(early Sep-late Dec)

40 lbs. draw weight at 28 in.
draw length minimum; 7/8 in.
width broadhead minimum

Illinois
    Deer-(early Oct-end Dec)
    Turkey-Limited (mid Apr-
        early May & begin
        Oct-end Dec)

No bowhunting during
firearms-deer; 40 lb. draw weight
at 28 in. draw length minimum;
7/8 in. width broadhead (barbless
only) minimum

Indiana
    Deer-(mid Oct-mid Nov & Dec)

35 lb. draw weight at 28 in. draw
length minimum; 7/8 in. width
broadhead minimum; no
mechanical devices to lock
string in drawn position

Iowa
  Deer & Turkey-(begin Oct-   Broadheads only
      early Dec &
      late Dec-early Jan)
  Spring Gobbler-(mid-Apr-
      mid-May)

Kansas
  Deer & Turkey-(begin Oct-   45 lb. draw weight minimum;
      early Dec &   compounds not over 65% let-off;
      mid-end Dec)   no electronic and chemical
  Antelope-(9 days late Sep)   devices

Kentucky
  Deer-(early Oct-early Nov &   String-locking devices prohibited
      end Nov-mid Jan)   7/8 in. width broadhead minimum

Louisiana
  Deer-Varies by parish (early Oct- 30 lb. draw weight minimum;
      late Jan)   7/8 in. width broadhead (well-
  See regs   sharpened, metal) minimum

Maine
  Deer-(begin Oct-begin Nov)   7/8 in. width broadhead minimum
                                     bows must be able to cast arrow
                                     150 yd. minimum; no chemical
                                     poison or explosive tips

Maryland
  Whitetail & Sika Deer-(mid Sep-   7/8 in. width broadhead minimum
      late Nov &   30 lb. draw weight minimum
      early Dec-   no poison chemical or explosive tips
      end Jan)

Massachusetts
  Deer-(early-late Nov)   Recurves and longbow 40 lb
                                     draw weight at 28 in. draw
                                     length minimum; 7/8 in. width
                                     broadhead minimum & 1 1/2 in.
                                     width broadhead maximum;
                                     mechanical releases allowed with
                                     handicap permit

Michigan
  Deer-(begin Oct-mid Nov)   Bows must be hand-held and
  Bear-(mid Sep-mid Oct)   hand-drawn

Minnesota
  Deer-(late Sep-end Dec)   40 lb. draw weight at/or before
                                     full draw minimum; 7/8 in.
                                     width broadhead (barbless,
                                     2 cutting edges) minimum

Mississippi
  Deer-(begin Oct-mid Nov)   No equipment restrictions

Missouri
Deer & Turkey-(early Oct-early
Nov & mid Nov-
end Dec)

Hand-held and hand-drawn
bows only

Montana
Deer & Elk-(early Sep-late Oct)
Antelope-(early Sep-mid Oct)

No poison or explosive tips

Nebraska
Deer & Antelope-(mid Sep-mid
Nov & late Nov-
end Dec)
Turkey-(early Mar-mid May
& begin Oct-early Nov)

40 lb. weight at 28 in. draw length
minimum; no electrical equipment
other than lighted pin sights, no
chemical or explosive tips; no
mechanical device to lock string in
drawn position

Nevada
Deer-(mid Aug-early Sep)
Antelope-(late Jul-mid Aug)
Elk-Resident only (Sep-Oct)

Bows must propel 400 gr. arrow
150 yd. (on level ground) minimum;
3/4 in. width broadhead minimum

New Hampshire
Deer-(mid Sep-mid Dec)

40 lb. draw weight minimum;
7/8 in. width broadhead minimum;
hunter's name and address on
arrows

New Jersey
Deer-(late Sep-early Nov &
early-late Jan)
Zone permit only (early
Nov-early Dec)

All bows except compounds 35
lb. draw weight at archer's draw
length minimum

New Mexico
Deer-(late Aug-late Sep & early-
mid Jan)
Barbary Sheep-Statewide (late
Jan)
By area (begin
Apr-end Mar)
Turkey-(late Apr-early May &
late Sep-early Oct)
Bear-(begin-end Apr & begin
Sep-end Dec)
Cougar-(begin Dec-end Mar)
Elk-(end Aug-late Sep)
Antelope-(early-late Aug)

Bows must propel arrows 160
yd. (on level ground) minimum;
broadheads must have sharpened
edges; no telescopic sights

New York
  Deer-North Zone (late Sep-
      mid Oct)
    South Zone (mid Oct-
      mid Nov)
  Bear-North Zone (mid Sep-
      mid Oct)
    South Zone (mid Oct-
      mid Nov)

Bow must cast arrow at 150 yd. minimum; 7/8 in. width broadhead (barbless) minimum; no mechanical draws attached to bow

North Carolina
  Deer-By Zones (early Sep-
      mid Nov)

45 lb. draw weight minimum; 7/8 in. width broadhead (barbless) minimum; only broadheads that cannot open upon impact may be used on big game; blunts may be used for birds & small game; no poisons or drugs

North Dakota
  Deer-(end Aug-end Dec)
  Antelope-(end Aug-late Oct)
  Bighorn Sheep-Residents only
      (late Sep-late Oct)

  Moose & Elk-Residents only
      (mid Sep-mid Oct)

Bows must be pulled & released by hand & cast arrow 130 yd. minimum; 24 in. arrow length 3/4 in. width & 1 1/2 in. length broadhead (2 cutting edges, long tipped & barbless) minimum; no electronic devices including stationary lighted sight pins

Ohio
  Deer-(early Oct-end Jan)

40 lb. draw weight minimum; 7/8 in. length broadhead (2 non-moving exposed cutting edges) minimum; no poison or explosive tips; no laser sights

Oklahoma
  Deer-(begin Oct-mid Nov &
      December)

All bows 40 lb. draw weight minimum; compounds with no more than 65% let-off; no laser sights & electronic tracking devices; 7/8 in. length broadhead minimum; no mechanical device to lock string in draw position

Oregon
  Deer-(late Aug-late Sep)

7/8 in. width broadhead (barbless, fixed position) minimum; 65% letoff at full draw maximum; no electronic devices or devices supported by bow to maintain at full draw

Pennsylvania
  Deer-(late Sep-late Oct &
    late Dec-mid Jan)

Long, recurve & compound
bows & arrows of cutting-edge
design; no poison or drug tips

Rhode Island
  Deer-Mainland (begin Oct-
    end Jan)
    Islands (begin Nov-
    end Jan)

40 lb. draw weight minimum;
7/8 in. width broadhead
minimum; no mechanical
releases; arrows must carry
hunter's name and address

South Carolina
  Deer-Varies (early Sep-
    begin Jan)

No equipment restrictions

South Dakota
  Deer-(begin Oct-end Dec)
  Antelope-(mid Aug-end Oct)

40 lb. draw weight minimum;
7/8 in. width broadhead (steel)
minimum; 9/16 in. width blunt
minimum

Tennessee
  Deer-By units (end Sep-mid Oct)

24 in. length arrow (big game)
minimum; 7/8 in. width broadhead
(sharpened steel, barbless, non-
expanding) minimum; bows must
propel arrow 150 yd.

Texas
  Deer & Turkey-(Oct)

40 lb. draw weight minimum;
7/8 in. width broadhead (2 cutting
edges) minimum; no field points
for small game.

Utah
  Deer-(mid Aug-early Sep)
  Elk-(begin-mid Sep)
  Antelope-See regs (end Aug-
    mid Sep)
  Moose-(end Aug-early Sep)

40 lb. draw weight minimum;
7/8 in. width broadhead minimum

Vermont
  Deer & Turkey-(early-late Oct)

7/8 in. width broadhead (2 cutting
edges) minimum

Virginia
  Deer & Bear-(mid Oct-mid Nov)
  See regs

Bows must propel arrow 125 yd.
minimum; 7/8 in. width broadhead
minimum

Washington
  Deer-By areas (mid Sep-early Oct)
  Elk-See regs (late Sep-early Feb)

40 lb. draw weight minimum; 400
gr. arrow weight minimum; 7/8 in.
width broadhead minimum; no
electrical device may be attached to
bow or device to hold at full draw

West Virginia
Deer & Boar-(mid Oct-
end Dec)
Bear-(mid Oct-late Nov)

3/4 in. width broadhead (2 sharp
edges) minimum

Wisconsin
Deer-(mid Sep-mid-Nov &
begin-end Dec)

30 lb. draw weight minimum;
7/8 in. width broadhead minimum;
no poison or drug tips

Wyoming
Deer & Elk-(begin-end Sep)
Antelope-(mid Aug-end Sep)
Other big game-(15 days before
gun season)

40 lb. draw weight & must cast 400
gr. arrow 160 yd. minimum; for
moose & elk 50 lb. draw weight or
must cast 500 gr. arrow 160 yd.
minimum; 1 in. width broadhead
minimum

Canada

Alberta
Deer, Elk & Moose-By zones
(early Sep-
end Nov)
Trophy Sheep-See regs

40 lb. draw weight minimum; 24
in. length arrow minimum; hunter's
current wildlife certificate number
printed on shaft

British Columbia
Deer, Bear, Caribou,
Mountain Goat & Moose-
By regions (dates vary)
See regs

40 lb draw weight within archer's
draw length minimum; 7/8 in.
width broadhead minimum

Manitoba
Big game by units
Deer-(late Aug-end Nov)
Moose-(late Aug-mid Oct)
Elk-(late Aug-mid Nov)

Guide for nonresident big game
hunters; 40 lb. draw weight at
28 in. draw length minimum;
7/8 inch width broadhead minimum

New Brunswick
Deer-(early-late Oct)
Bear-(early-late Sep)

20 mm. width broadhead
(barbless) minimum; 20 kg.
draw weight at 70 cm. draw length
minimum; no explosive tips

Newfoundland/Labrador
Moose-By zones (late Aug-Dec)
Bear-By zones (late Aug-Dec)

20 kg. draw weight at full draw
length minimum; 2 metal cutting
edges broadhead minimum

Nova Scotia
Deer-(begin-mid Oct)

50 lb. for moose & 40 lb. for deer
draw weight minimums; blaze
orange required of all bowhunters

Northwest Territories
  No special seasons

20 kg. draw weight at 700 mm. draw length minimum; 25 mm. width broadhead (barbless) minimum; no explosive points

Prince Edward Island
  No special seasons

No equipment restrictions

Ontario
  No special seasons

40 lb. draw weight except 44 lb. for moose and bear draw weight minimums; 24 in. arrow length minimum; 7/8 in. width broadhead (2 sharp, non-serrated, barbless) minimum

Quebec
  Moose-By zone (late Aug-Oct)
  Deer-By zone (late Sep-Oct)

40 lb. draw weight at 28 in. draw length minimum; 7/8 in. width broadhead minimum

Saskatchewan
  Deer-(early Sep-mid Oct)
  Antelope-Residents Only
        (early Sep-mid Oct)
  Elk-Residents Only
     (late Aug-early Sep)
  Moose-Residents Only
     (late Sep-early Oct)

40 lb. draw weight minimum; 7/8 in. width broadhead minimum; no poison, drug or explosive tips

Yukon Territory
  No special seasons; See regs
  for special archery areas

45 lb. draw weight minimum; 28 in. length arrow minimum; broadheads required